"Blessed art thou, Simon Bar-Jona, for flesh and blood has not revealed this to thee, but my Father in heaven.

And I say to thee, thou art Peter, and upon this rock I will build my Church, and the gates of hell shall not prevail against it.

And I will give thee the keys of the Kingdom of heaven; and whatever thou shalt bind on earth shall be bound in heaven and whatever thou shalt loose on earth shall be loosed in heaven."

—Matthew 16: 17–19

Foreword by Cardinal Seán O'Malley was adapted from his blog, Cardinal Seán's Blog (www.cardinalseansblog.org).
Used with permission.

Papal homilies © Libreria Editrice. All rights reserved.
Used with permission.

Cover and interior design by Chris Pelicano

Cataloging-in-Publication data on file with the Library of Congress

ISBN: 978-1-61890-136-1

Published in the United States by
Saint Benedict Press, LLC
PO Box 410487
Charlotte, NC 28241
www.saintbenedictpress.com

Printed and bound in the United States of America

Saint Benedict Press, LLC
Charlotte, North Carolina
2013

POPE FRANCIS

The Pope from the End of the Earth

POPE FRANCIS

The Pope from the End of the Earth

Thomas J. Craughwell

Foreword by
Cardinal Seán O'Malley

SAINT
BENEDICT
PRESS

TABLE OF CONTENTS

JORGE MARIO BERGOGLIO
Biographical Timeline of Pope Francis

1936

On December 17, 1936 Jorge Mario Bergoglio is born in Buenos Aires, Argentina, to Mario and Regina Sivori Bergoglio, Italian immigrants.

1957

Physicians find cysts on one of Bergoglio's lungs. To save his life, surgeons remove a portion of the affected lung.

1958

Enters the Jesuit novitiate.

1960

Takes his vows in the Society of Jesus.

1960–1963

Studies philosophy and humanities as part of his seminary training.

1964–1966

Teaches literature and psychology to high school students in Santa Fe and Buenos Aires.

1967–1970

Studies theology at the Colegio de San Jose in San Miguel.

1969

Ordained a priest of the Society of Jesus.

1970–1971

Completes his tertianship, his final training as a Jesuit, at Alcala de Henares in Spain.

1973

Makes his perpetual vows as a Jesuit.

1973

Elected provincial, or superior, of the Jesuits in Argentina.

1976

During Argentina's Dirty War, two Jesuits priests, Fathers Franz Jalics and Orlando Yorio, are seized by the military. Working behind the scenes, Father Bergoglio manages to win their release.

1980–1986

Serves as rector of the Colegio de San Jose.

1986

Travels to Germany to complete his doctoral thesis.

1992

Receives his episcopal ordination as auxiliary archbishop of Buenos Aires and titular bishop of Auca.

1997

Named coadjutor bishop with the right to succeed.

1998

Consecrated archbishop of Buenos Aires.

2000

Visits the deathbed of former bishop Jeronimo Podesta and befriends Podesta's wife, Clelia Luro.

2001

Elevated to cardinal by Pope John Paul II.

2005–2011

Serves as president of the Argentine Bishops Conference, after turning down the appointment in 2002.

2005

Took part in the conclave that elected Pope Benedict XVI and is widely believed to have finished second in the balloting.

2010

Opposes the government's policy of legalizing same-sex marriage. The bill passes in spite of Cardinal Bergoglio's efforts.

2013

Elected pope; takes the name "Francis," in honor of St. Francis of Assisi.

Foreword

FOR CATHOLICS—and Catholics from the Americas in particular—the Holy Father is a great blessing. Pope Francis is the first pope from the American hemisphere and, being Hispanic, he is from a part of the world where almost half of all Catholics reside. He is a man who has been very much dedicated to the poor and announcing the Gospel in difficult situations. We know he will be a great blessing for our Church.

It was my privilege to visit him a couple years ago. I had met him in different meetings over the years and when I made a trip to South America for the United States Bishops Conference to visit projects in Paraguay that are funded by the collection for Latin America, I stopped in Argentina on the way, where I was his guest and we had a wonderful visit. On that occasion, he gave me a beautiful recording of the *Missa Criolla*, the Argentine Mass.

I did not encounter him again until we cardinals gathered in Rome to elect the new pope.

Just before the conclave began, we went to the Domus Sanctae Marthae (Latin for Saint Martha's House) where we were sequestered for the duration of the conclave. That afternoon, we went to the Pauline Chapel where we prayed and then processed into the Sistine Chapel, chanting the Litany of Saints.

When we arrived at the Sistine Chapel there were more prayers. We received a second meditation from Maltese Cardinal Prospero Grech. Then we had the first *scrutinium*, or scrutiny, as the vote is called. The first scrutiny was inconclusive so the ballots were burnt and the black smoke was visible Tuesday night.

On Wednesday, we went once again from the Domus Sanctae Marthae to the Sistine Chapel where we had prayers and two scrutinies in the morning.

Each cardinal went up by order of seniority. Before placing his ballot in the receptacle on the altar, each cardinal took a vow—standing before Michelangelo's scene of the Last Judgment—calling on Christ to witness that we would only vote for the person we felt God really wanted for the office of Holy Father. It is a very moving experience.

Neither of those two scrutinies were conclusive.

Between the morning and afternoon gatherings we went back to the Domus Sanctae Marthae. Cardinal Bergoglio and I sat together for lunch. I could see he was under a lot of pressure at that point, and he did not eat much!

In the afternoon, we returned to the Sistine Chapel for more prayers. We had two more scrutinies, and on the second vote the Holy Father was elected.

It was a very emotional and moving moment when Cardinal Bergoglio accepted his election and announced that his name would be Francis in honor of Saint Francis of Assisi. He said very explicitly that he was taking the name after St. Francis of Assisi. As a Jesuit, it would have been understandable if he had chosen the name in honor of St. Francis Xavier, who is one of the greatest missionaries in the history of the Church, but he specified that he was taking the name after St. Francis of Assisi.

Without having discussed it with the Holy Father, I think that there are some themes from the life of St. Francis that he is trying to communicate by choosing this name.

One of the themes of Francis's life is the call to rebuild the Church, which is a call to reform, and to deepen our conversion to the Lord. Another theme would be Francis's theme of universal brotherhood; of making a world where we are brothers and sisters to each other. Saint Francis, of course, saw himself as a brother to all of creation and to everyone.

Saint Francis also had a special love for the poor, who are a sacrament of the crucified Christ. The Holy Father, in his ministry as archbishop, has been so dedicated to the poorest of the poor. I think we will see a continuation of that in his pontificate.

After Pope Francis announced his name, each of the cardinals went up, kissed his ring and greeted him. Afterwards, we prayed the *Te Deum*, the traditional Catholic prayer of thanksgiving, and the Holy Father was taken away, vested in his white vestments, to pray privately in the chapel.

It was then that the ballots were burnt, and the white smoke and bells announced to the city of Rome and to the world that the new Holy Father had been elected.

We then went to the loggia overlooking the Piazza of St. Peter's accompanying the Holy Father.

Looking out onto St. Peter's square from the balcony was an impressive sight, with thousands of people cheering, waving flags, and taking pictures. The energy of the crowd was incredible when they saw the Holy Father for the first time.

He gave a warm and simple greeting to the people and asked for prayers for Pope Benedict and then asked for a moment of silence and asked for the people to pray for God's blessing upon him. He led the people in the Our Father, the Hail Mary, and the Glory Be. This, for me, was a very moving moment because it occurred to me that these very simple prayers are the ones that every Catholic knows, whether they be illiterate or a rocket scientist, whether they are children or elderly. These are the prayers that unite us as a Catholic people in our life of faith and worship of God.

In the days after the election of our new Holy Father I remained in Rome waiting for the feast of St. Joseph and the inaugural Mass, and was able to see Pope Francis's service to the people of God up close. It has become clear that the Holy Father's simplicity, his love for the poor, and his accessibility are going to be hallmarks of his papacy.

Even the way he celebrates the Mass is much more like the parish Masses that our Catholic people are used to experiencing in their local churches. At Santa Anna, where he celebrated Mass on Sunday for the local parish of Vatican City, he greeted people at the door, the way that pastors have done in the United States since I was a young priest.

Certainly we see the Holy Father's intention is to be close to the people. This was made even more apparent when Pope Francis announced that he would celebrate the Mass of the Lord's Supper on Holy Thursday in a Roman prison and wash the feet of some of the young detainees, as an occasion to underscore the Church's commitment and preferential love for the poor.

Holy Thursday is a very fitting time for that and we have a very long history of that in the Church. I recall that in England during the Middle Ages, the king would wash the feet of beggars and give each one of them a gold coin on Maundy Thursday.

One year, we did something similar at the Cathedral in Boston, bringing people from Pine Street Inn to have their feet washed at the Holy Thursday liturgy.

In the Church, there has often been an association of Christ's commandment that we love one another as directed in a very special way to the sick and to the poor. That was ritualized in Holy Thursday ceremonies, and I was very touched that our Holy Father wished to emphasize that again.

Finally, the cardinals and Catholics in Rome and around the world again gathered in common prayer as Pope Francis held his inaugural Mass on the feast of Saint Joseph.

The weather was beautiful during the Mass which was held outside, in front of Saint Peter's. It was a miraculously picture-perfect moment given to us by St. Joseph, because it was raining both before and after the Mass.

Saint Joseph has always been a very important part of my life and so during the Mass I remembered the Mosaic of St. Joseph with the two turtledoves that I saw at the Irish College the day before. It is a portrayal of St. Joseph not often seen, but I like it very much. At the Presentation, our Blessed Mother would have been carrying Jesus, so Joseph would have been in charge of the doves.

Jewish law dictated that first-born children were dedicated to God, a reminder of the first-born children spared by the Passover of the Angel. When presenting their first-born children at the Temple, Jewish families were supposed to sacrifice a lamb. But the law said that if you were poor, you could sacrifice two turtledoves instead. Mary and Joseph were poor people, and so they made the sacrifice of the turtledoves.

I thought the homily was so beautifully put, with the Holy Father calling upon us to be, like Joseph, guardians and to take care of creation, of each other, and in particular the poor. He spoke about how parents take care of children and then, later, the children take care of their parents. It was a very beautiful pro-life theme. We are the people of life: we take care of the child in the womb, we take care of the newborn baby, and then we take care of the elderly and those who have died.

For us, as Catholics, the selection of the pope is very important. The decision of Pope Benedict to retire was, in some ways, a crisis and so the election of the new Holy Father is a great consolation to the Catholic people with its sense of continuity in the Church.

We have been so blessed in the last century and a half with so many exceptional and holy men who have led us in the Catholic Church, though each of them was so different from the one who came before. I think that is what we see here. Someone told me the Italians have an expression— "After a fat Pope, a thin Pope" —which shows that each one is different and each one has different gifts that they bring to their ministry in the Church.

I am sure that Pope Francis, just as Pope Benedict, will share with us the wonderful gifts and talents that God has given him to be put at the service of God's people.

This book serves as a glimpse into those talents and gifts that our new pope possesses. It is a beautiful encounter—in pictures and in words—with Pope Francis, from his early life to those anxious days when the Church awaited its new pope, to the joy of his election and the days that followed.

Viva il Papa!

—Cardinal Seán O'Malley, OFM Cap.
Archbishop of Boston

Habemus Papam!

AT 7:05 P.M., ROME TIME, a large puff of smoke billowed out from the temporary chimney on the roof of the Sistine Chapel.

The smoke was dark gray. At first, some viewers in the crowd at Saint Peter's Square thought it was once again black, a sign that in the fifth ballot the cardinals still had not elected a pope. But as more smoke spilled out of the chimney it became apparent that this time the color was white.

As jubilation swept through the crowd, the bells of St. Peter's began to ring. The pealing of bells spread from church to church, until all Rome was clanging with the happy sound. The crowd took up the chants, *"Viva il papa!"* (Long live the pope!) and *"Habemus papam!"* (We have a pope!).

Romans and visitors descended on St. Peter's Square. A crowd numbering in the tens of thousands packed the piazza, and the overflow spilled down the Via della Conciliazione, the broad boulevard that leads to St. Peter's.

It had been a cold, raw, rainy day, and the weather was no better in the evening. Nonetheless, the vast crowd remained excited and eager as they waited to discover who would follow Benedict XVI as the Successor of Peter and head of the 1.2 billion–member Roman Catholic Church.

After nearly an hour Cardinal Jean-Louis Pierre Tauran, the senior cardinal-deacon, stepped onto the balcony above the main entrance of St. Peter's Basilica. *"Annuntio vobis gaudium magnum. Habemus papam!"* he declared. "I announce to you a great joy. We have a pope! His Most Eminent and Reverend Lord, Jorge Cardinal Bergoglio, who has chosen for himself the name Francis."

The popular American blogger, Father John Zuhlsdorf, a.k.a. Father Z, posted later that for a moment the crowd was quiet. In the hours and days before this moment, the crowd and the world had been avidly discussing the *papabili*—the cardinals thought likely to be elected pope. But they didn't recognize the name Bergoglio. He had not figured in their discussions, and initially only a small number of Argentinian pilgrims whooped with delight.

Bergoglio had been a strong contender in the previous conclave, and he was widely believed to have been runner-up to Benedict XVI. But this time around he had largely fallen off the radar screen. At seventy-six many had dismissed him as too old.

Perhaps the most surprised and happiest man in the piazza was Sergio Rubin, a reporter for Argentina's Catholic newspaper, *Clarin*. Rubin had authored Cardinal Bergoglio's biography, *El Jesuita (The Jesuit)*. Reporting on live television from St. Peter's Square, an excited Rubin told viewers, "An Argentinian pope—it is an enormous surprise to all of us!"

Rubin continued:

> He was a candidate last time, but we didn't expect him to be one this time because of his age. But he is the new pope— an Argentinian! . . . Cardinal Jorge Bergoglio, now Pope

Francis—the first Francis. So, it is the first time a Pope has taken this name. That means he wants to give a message: the message of Saint Francis, a man who arrived to the Church in a great moment of opulence, bringing with him humility and love for the poor to revitalize the Church, to give some fresh air. Just now, the Church needs that fresh air and revitalization.

A few minutes later, the double doors swung open again. This time it was the new pope who stepped out.

Francis seemed a bit hesitant, perhaps even shy. As the throng erupted, he raised his hand and gave a little wave. He was dressed only in the white papal cassock. He had declined to wear the traditional red velvet, ermine-lined mozzetta. The richly embroidered stole, also part of the traditional garb of a pope-elect, was in the hands of Monsignor Guido Marini, the master of papal liturgical ceremonies.

Then Francis began to speak:

Brothers and sisters good evening! You all know that the duty of the conclave was to give a bishop to Rome. It seems

that my brother Cardinals have gone almost to the ends of the earth to get him . . . but here we are. I thank you for the welcome that has come from the diocesan community of Rome.

After this informal greeting, Francis's thoughts and prayers turned to his predecessor. "First of all I would like to say a prayer for our Bishop Emeritus Benedict XVI. Let us all pray together for him, that the Lord will bless him and that our Lady will protect him." Together the pope and the crowd recited the Our Father, the Hail Mary, and the Glory Be.

Francis continued:

And now let us begin this journey, the Bishop and the people, this journey of the Church of Rome which presides in charity over all the Churches, a journey of brotherhood in love, of mutual trust.

Let us always pray for one another. Let us pray for the whole world that there might be a great sense of brotherhood. My hope is that this journey of the Church that we begin today, together with the help of my Cardinal Vicar, may be fruitful for the evangelization of this beautiful city.

And now I would like to give the blessing. But first I want to ask you a favor. Before the Bishop blesses the people I ask that you would pray to the Lord to bless me—the prayer of the people for their Bishop. Let us say this prayer—your prayer for me—in silence.

Then Francis bowed, bending almost double. The crowd fell silent and begged God's blessing on their new pope and bishop.

When he raised himself up, Francis took the stole, kissed it, and draped it over his shoulders. "I will now give my blessing to you and to the whole world, to all men and women of good will." Francis then delivered the *Urbi et Orbi* blessing, a special prayer for the people gathered before the pope and for the Church throughout the world:

> *Sancti Apostoli Petrus et Paulus: de quorum potestate et auctoritate confidimus ipsi intercedant pro nobis ad Dominum.*
>
> *Precibus et meritis beatæ Mariae semper Virginis, beati Michaelis Archangeli, beati Ioannis Baptistæ, et sanctorum Apostolorum Petri et Pauli et omnium Sanctorum misereatur vestri omnipotens Deus; et dimissis omnibus peccatis vestris, perducat vos Iesus Christus ad vitam æternam.*
>
> *Indulgentiam, absolutionem et remissionem omnium peccatorum vestrorum, spatium verae et fructuosae poenitentiæ, cor semper penitens, et emendationem vitae, gratiam et consolationem Sancti Spiritus; et finalem perseverantiam in bonis operibus tribuat vobis omnipotens et misericors Dominus.*
>
> *Et benedictio Dei omnipotentis, Patris et Filii et Spiritus Sancti descendat super vos et maneat semper.*

May the Holy Apostles Peter and Paul, in whose power and authority we have confidence, intercede on our behalf to the Lord.

Through the prayers and merits of the Blessed Mary ever-virgin, of Blessed Michael the Archangel, of Blessed John the Baptist, and of the Holy Apostles Peter and Paul, and of all the saints, may Almighty God have mercy on you, and with your sins forgiven, may Jesus Christ lead you into everlasting life.

Why Does the Pope Change His Name?

Our first pope, Peter, took a name other than his own when Christ instituted the Church and the Papacy. However, he did not change it of his own accord, but rather, Christ assigned him a new name. In scripture, a name change signaled a change in status, and certainly Peter's status changed when he was put in charge of the Church.

The first pope—after Peter—to change his name was John II in 533. His given name was Mercury, and he felt it unsuitable for a pope to bear the name of a pagan god. He chose "John" in honor of Pope St. John I, who had died a martyr just seven years earlier.

Four hundred and fifty years passed before another pope changed his name. In 983 a man named Peter was elected pope. Uncomfortable with the thought of being addressed as Peter II, he took the name John XIV. Since then every newly elected pope (with two exceptions) has adopted a new name.

May the Almighty and merciful Lord grant you indulgence, absolution, and remission of all your sins, time for a true and fruitful penance, an always repentant heart and amendment of life, the grace and consolation of the Holy Spirit, and final perseverance in good works.

And may the blessing of Almighty God, the Father, the Son, and the Holy Spirit, descend on you and remain with you always.

After giving his blessing, Francis removed the stole, kissed it again, and handed it back to Monsignor Marini. "Brothers and sisters, I am leaving you," he said. "Thank you for your welcome. Pray for me and I will be with you again soon. We will see one another soon. Tomorrow I want to go to pray to the Madonna, that she may protect Rome. Good night and sleep well!" Then Pope Francis stepped through the open doorway, into the loggia of St. Peter's.

The pope's car and driver were waiting to take him to the Domus Sanctae Marthae (the House of Saint Martha). But Francis surprised the driver and the world when he said he would take the shuttle bus with some of his cardinals instead.

As the cardinals went to a festive dinner with the pope they had just elected, the world tried to get a grip on the man who had become the 266th pope. There was a lot to take in. Francis was the first pope from the New World. He was a Latin American—a significant fact given that 42 percent of the Catholic faithful live in Latin America. He had chosen a name that no pope had ever taken—Francis, after the great saint of Assisi. And he was a Jesuit—another first, for the papacy and the Society of Jesus, the Catholic religious order founded by St. Ignatius of Loyola in 1540.

Perhaps the most striking thing, however, about the newly elected

Pope Francis was his deep humility. The choice of the name Francis was significant. In an attempt to imitate Jesus Christ as closely as possible, St. Francis of Assisi had taken upon himself a life of absolute poverty, humility, and charity. The great saint was also famously exhorted by the crucified Christ in a vision, "Francis, rebuild my Church, which has fallen into ruins."

Early the next morning Pope Francis made a pilgrimage to the Basilica of Saint Mary Major. He went to pray before an icon of the Virgin and Child known as *Salus Populi Romani*, Protectress of the Roman People—the most beloved, most venerated image of the Blessed Mother in the Eternal City.

Francis had brought along a small flower arrangement. He placed it upon the altar, then he knelt down and prayed for a full half hour. Next he went to pray before the relics of the Manger, then at the altar where St. Ignatius of Loyola, the founder of the Jesuits, offered his first Mass. His final stop was at the tomb of Pope St. Pius V, known for implementing the reforms of the Council of Trent, including a vigorous reform of the hierarchy.

The Italian newspaper *La Repubblica* reported that Pope Francis had given the staff of St. Mary Major only ten minutes warning of his visit. He also instructed them not to close the basilica while he was there. "I'm a pilgrim, and I just want to be one among the pilgrims," he reportedly said. The staff closed the church anyway. With his visit to St. Mary Major concluded, Francis was driven to his hotel, where he again surprised his retinue by collecting his luggage himself and paying his own hotel bill.

Pope Francis's low-key, down-to-earth manner and his off-the-cuff remarks from the balcony of St. Peter's charmed the media. One news outlet after another reported that as Archbishop of Buenos Aires Cardinal Bergoglio had lived in a modest apartment instead of the archbishop's palace, had ridden the bus and subway to work, and cooked his own meals.

Even as Francis prayed at St. Mary Major, all eyes were on the pope's feet: would he wear the custom-made red loafers Benedict XVI favored? The answer was "no." Pope Francis walked up the aisle of the basilica in black shoes, simple though brand new. Two South American priests told the British newspaper the *Telegraph* that Cardinal Bergoglio's shoes were so shabby that friends bought him a new pair so he would look respectable at the conclave.

Just days before, this humble man from South America had left his modest apartment for the conclave, wearing shoes he had received as a gift. Now he donned them as papal footwear as he prayed in front of Our Lady as pope. Indeed, he had worn them the night before as he looked out over the people he would lead.

Let us take a look at the events within the Church that brought this man from "the end of the earth" to the center of the most prominent balcony in the most famous and important square in Christendom. Just a month prior, Benedict XVI shocked Catholics and the

world by announcing his resignation, and now Rome welcomed its new bishop, and the Church welcomed its new shepherd.

When Jorge Mario Bergoglio—Pope Francis—walked through the doors and out onto the balcony of St. Peter's, he finally ended a time of uncertainty and anxiety for Catholics around the world.

Benedict Resigns

AS A BELL TOLLED eight times, two Swiss Guards closed the tall wooden doors of Castel Gandolfo, the papal residence outside Rome. Then they surrendered their command to three Vatican gendarmes. It was 8:00 p.m., February 28, 2013. Benedict XVI's resignation was now complete.

The Swiss Guards' sole duty is to protect the pope. Since the Catholic Church now had no pope the guards were furloughed until Benedict's successor was elected. It was a low-key conclusion to an event the world had not witnessed for nearly six hundred years.

Two weeks earlier, on February 11, 2013, the feast of Our Lady of Lourdes, the world awoke to stunning news: Pope Benedict XVI would resign the papacy effective February 28. Benedict had made his announcement during a meeting with a group of cardinals, ostensibly to canonize three new saints. Speaking in Latin, Benedict told the gathering:

> After having repeatedly examined my conscience before God,
> I have come to the certainty that my strengths, due to an

advanced age, are no longer suited to an adequate exercise of the Petrine ministry . . . For this reason, and well aware of the seriousness of this act, with full freedom I declare that I renounce the ministry of Bishop of Rome, Successor of Saint Peter, entrusted to me by the Cardinals on 19 April 2005, in such a way, that as from 28 February 2013, at 20:00 hours, the See of Rome, the See of Saint Peter, will be vacant and a Conclave to elect the new Supreme Pontiff will have to be convoked by those whose competence it is.

Benedict's announcement came as a shock. No pope had resigned since 1415, and even Benedict's inner circle had no inkling of what he was planning to do. The pope's spokesman, Father Federico Lombardi, told reporters, "This announcement has taken us all by surprise." Father Lombardi went on to say that Benedict's closest aides were "incredulous."

"His age is weighing on him," Father Georg Ratzinger, the pope's brother, explained to reporters. "At this age my brother wants more rest."

As Benedict retired to the lakeside papal retreat at Castel Gandolfo, the Church entered an unusual period: *sede vacante*—the chair is empty. For a time, the Church would be without a pope; without a leader here on earth.

For Catholics, the *sede vacante* period is a time of uncertainty, anxiety, and excitement all at once. It is also a time of reflection: a time to reflect on the previous pope, the state of the Church, and the direction it is headed.

As is true of any pope, Benedict XVI's legacy is complex. He was a first-class intellectual and a great teaching pope, who time and again revealed to the modern world how faith and reason are inextricably linked. He advanced "the hermeneutic of continuity" with regard to

how the documents of Vatican II are to be interpreted, answering decades-old arguments that Vatican II was a rupture—a complete break with—the "old Church" and the coming-to-be of a new one.

Benedict inaugurated a streamlined process that welcomed traditionalist Anglicans into the Catholic Church. He liberated the Latin Mass, now known as the Extraordinary Form of the Mass. Whereas priests previously had required the special permission of their bishop to say the Latin Mass, Benedict decreed in the Apostolic Letter *Summorum Pontificum* that all priests have the right to say the Latin Mass on their own accord. The faithful were free to attend—and did so in growing numbers. During the eight years of Benedict's pontificate, the number of Latin Masses offered by the Roman Catholic Church in the United States nearly doubled, reaching over four hundred Latin Masses today.

Benedict did not say Mass in the Extraordinary Form himself. But his Masses were marked by reverence and solemnity. He included in his liturgies more Gregorian chant, more classical sacred music, and made use once again of magnificent pre-Vatican II vestments.

He required that those who received Communion from him do so kneeling and receiving on the tongue. One of his deepest desires as pope was to heal the rupture with the Society of St. Pius X, the Catholic traditionalist movement founded in 1970 by breakaway French archbishop Marcel Lefebvre. Unfortunately it was not to be.

Another key challenge Benedict faced as pope was addressing the sexual abuse crisis. Arguably his most dramatic act in this regard was ordering an investigation of Father Marcial Maciel, founder of the Legion of Christ. The investigators discovered that Maciel had fathered at least three children and sexually abused an untold number of underage seminarians. Based on the initial results of the investigation, Benedict removed Maciel from active ministry in 2006. In 2010, after the full conclusion of the investigation, the Vatican formally denounced Maciel. By that time, Maciel was dead, but Benedict had the courage to bring to completion a painful inquiry into one of the most popular groups within the Church in order to uphold morality and justice. Benedict appointed Archbishop (now Cardinal) Velasio de Paolis, C.S., to take charge of the Legion and reform it.

Benedict's attempts to introduce the concept of transparency to Vatican finances and to break down the bureaucracy of the Curia had mixed results. Nonetheless, it was a healthy sign when a pope invited outside auditors to study the Vatican's books. Furthermore, he successfully appointed men of integrity to top posts in the Curia.

As one would expect from a man who for twenty-four years led the Congregation for the Doctrine of the Faith, Benedict was no friend of heterodoxy. During his papacy, the orders of sisters and nuns who belonged to the Leadership Conference for Women Religious in the United States were instructed to reform themselves; liberal theologians were censured; and Maryknoll priest, Father Roy Bourgeois, was excommunicated for his outspoken and public support of women's ordination.

In the days before the conclave, as the world turned its attention to a Church in transition, one thing became clear: despite Benedict's good and holy work as pope, the challenges that would face the new pope remained daunting. The sex abuse crisis is still with us and its ramifications will last for years. And a report on the Curia, commissioned by Benedict and delivered to him shortly before he resigned, revealed that the Church's administration is rife with careerism, cronyism, and factionalism.

As secularism in Europe and North America becomes more aggressive, the Church increasingly finds itself on the defensive. Weekly Mass attendance by Catholics in the United States is down to 23 percent. In Europe it is worse: 4.5 percent in France, 15 percent in Italy, 15 percent in Spain. The reconversion of Europe and America—John Paul II's "New Evangelization"—has never been more urgent.

In addition to secularism and the reform of the Curia, other challenges remain. Russell Shaw, blogging for *Our Sunday Visitor* before Francis's election, suggested that the new pope must also find solutions to the growing anti-Christian movements in Africa and the Middle East. In these lands Christian communities dating back to the time of the apostles are in danger of dying out, as Catholics and Orthodox leave their homelands and emigrate to countries where they can practice their faith freely.

Shaw also suggested that the new pope must have strong, convincing answers to those dissident Catholics calling for women priests, abortion-and-contraception-on-demand, same sex marriage, and greatly reducing the authority of the pope and the bishops. These dissidents are often given prominence by the secular media. Many have even found a platform in Church institutions, including Catholic colleges and universities. Answering this heterodox vision

What Can the Pope Do?

Few people, even among Catholics, realize that the papacy is the oldest institution in the world. The dustbin of history—to borrow Leon Trotsky's famous phrase—is heaped high with the empires, kingdoms, social and political movements that the popes have seen come and go. The Roman Caesars, the barbarian invaders, the Holy Roman Emperors, the Reign of Terror, the Third Reich, and the Soviet Empire are all gone, but there is still a pope in Rome.

The pope is the last word on all points of doctrine, but he is bound by precedents, or what the Church calls "the deposit of faith." This "deposit" includes everything God has revealed to humankind about Himself, and what Jesus Christ and His apostles taught.

No pope has the authority to deny such points of doctrine as the bodily resurrection of Christ, or the Real Presence of Jesus in the consecrated bread and wine—to name just two. What he can do, however, is find ways to teach the ancient truths of the faith that are fresh and contemporary.

The pope also has the powers of a judge. In all decisions from Church courts, the pope is the final appeal—a one-man Supreme Court. For example, if a Church court concludes that what a Catholic theologian has been teaching is at variance with the doctrine of the Church, the theologian has the right to appeal to the pope, who may confirm or overturn the court's verdict. Once the pope has made up his mind, there is no further appeal.

The pope also is the temporal ruler of Vatican City, a sovereign city-state within the city of Rome. Vatican City has a population of about 800, and about 3,000 employees, almost all of whom work in

the Roman Curia, the administrative branch of the Catholic Church.

Finally, the pope is infallible in certain instances, a tenet of the faith that is often misunderstood. Simply put, the pope is infallible only when he draws upon his authority as supreme shepherd of the Church to teach or define some matter relating either to faith or morals. Such events are very rare. The last time a pope exercised his infallibility was 1950, when Pius XII declared that it was a doctrine of the Church that at the end of her earthly life, the Blessed Virgin Mary was assumed into Heaven, body and soul.

How did the popes acquire this authority? We find the answer in the gospels: "Blessed art thou, Simon Bar-Jona, for flesh and blood has not revealed this to thee, but my Father in heaven. And I say to thee, thou art Peter, and upon this rock I will build my Church, and the gates of hell shall not prevail against it. And I will give thee the keys of the Kingdom of heaven; and whatever thou shalt bind on earth shall be bound in heaven and whatever thou shalt loose on earth shall be loosed in heaven." (Matthew 16: 17-19)

of the Church, and putting forth in its stead what the great writer G. K. Chesterton called the "romance of orthodoxy," will be a key challenge for Pope Francis.

There is much work to be done here. But Francis benefits from the earlier work and initiatives not only of Benedict XVI, but also of John Paul II, perhaps the greatest evangelizer of modern times.

When John Paul II was elected pope in 1978, he inherited a Church that was facing challenges equal to, and perhaps graver than, the ones facing Francis today. Millions of Catholics and other Christians were trapped behind the "Iron Curtain," citizens of officially atheistic communist governments determined to stamp out Christianity as a threat to the state.

In the West, parishes and dioceses were implementing the decrees of the Second Vatican Council—often very poorly. In gross misinterpretations of the Council, Gregorian chant, sacred polyphony, and beautiful religious statuary seemed to disappear from parish life virtually overnight. Folk hymns and felt banners took their place. There was a palpable loss of a sense of the sacred. A loss of vocations followed. In the years after the Council, thousands left the priesthood, and the number of nuns in the United States dropped dramatically.

Furthermore, in the years following Vatican II, abuses of the Council and the new Mass by both the clergy and laity quickly shifted the focus away from Christ in the Eucharist. Due to an increasingly casual and sometimes irreverent attitude toward the Eucharist, combined with often lukewarm catechesis during these years, it is no surprise that in 1994 a *New York Times* and CBS poll found that 70 percent of American Catholics did not believe in the Real Presence.

But with the election of John Paul II, the first non-Italian Pope in 455 years, change was in the air. And slowly, bit by bit, John

Paul began to reverse the trend. He encouraged Catholics to pray the rosary. Every Good Friday, he led the Stations of the Cross in the Colosseum before enormous crowds, and with the television cameras rolling. He introduced Exposition of the Blessed Sacrament to St. Peter's Basilica, a practice which was adopted by cathedrals and parish churches around the globe, and served to revive devotion to the holy Eucharist. He revived the custom of the Corpus Christi procession. And he renewed devotion to the saints by canonizing and beatifying more than fifteen-hundred men, women, and children.

In 1994, John Paul authorized the publication of the *Catechism of the Catholic Church*, the first official catechism since the one published after the Council of Trent in the mid-sixteenth century. To reach young Catholics, he launched World Youth Day, a periodic gathering in which hundreds of thousands of Catholic youth from all over the world come together around the pope for several days of Masses, discussions, and instruction in the Catholic faith. Gradually, young people became interested in their religion, and some were inspired to enter the priesthood and religious life. Young men who entered the seminary at this time were known as "JP2 priests."

This foundation laid down by John Paul II was built upon by Benedict XVI. Now it is up to Francis to continue construction of this edifice that shows such promise.

In the four weeks between Benedict's resignation and the afternoon the cardinals filed into the Sistine Chapel, there was a great deal of speculation in the press about what issues the cardinals might believe to be most vital in the coming pontificate. John Allen of the *National Catholic Reporter* identified four topics he believed the cardinals had discussed before they went into the conclave: reforming the Vatican Curia or administration, adopting a pastoral approach to contemporary issues, reaching out to the Third World, and being more evangelical, more of a missionary, to the developing world and the increasingly secularized West.

Reform of the Curia: More than a few Rome-watchers think the Curia is broken, where squabbling between departments and curial officials undermines efficiency. Allen cites, as an example, the debacle of 2009, when Benedict lifted the excommunications of the four schismatic bishops of the Society of St. Pius X. One of these bishops was Richard Williamson, who had a notorious reputation—and a paper trail—as a Holocaust-denier. When the story broke, Benedict looked foolish. *Vaticanisti* who want the Curia reformed believe that staffers should have known about Williamson's obnoxious opinions and intervened before the fact to save the pope from being embarrassed.

Pastoral Sensitivity: A pope with a pastoral touch would address the complexities of contemporary issues while upholding the teachings of the Church. Allen himself offered an example: "Imagine two different answers from the new pope about gay marriage. Answer one: 'Assaults on the family are a moral cancer, and we must defend God's truth.' Answer two: 'Church teaching is well-known, but our desire is to reach out in a spirit of love.' It's the same content, but the feel is vastly different."

The Third World: The Catholic Church is growing at an explosive rate in Africa and Asia. Between 2005 and 2010, the Catholic population of Africa increased by 21 percent. The news is almost as good in Asia, where between 2000 and 2008, the number of Catholics increased by 15.6 percent. Such numbers suggest that the Church in Africa and Asia is well-established—a fact that inspired discussion before the conclave about electing a pope from the Third World.

Evangelization: John Paul II spearheaded the idea of reconverting the West, where too often religion is met with indifference if not

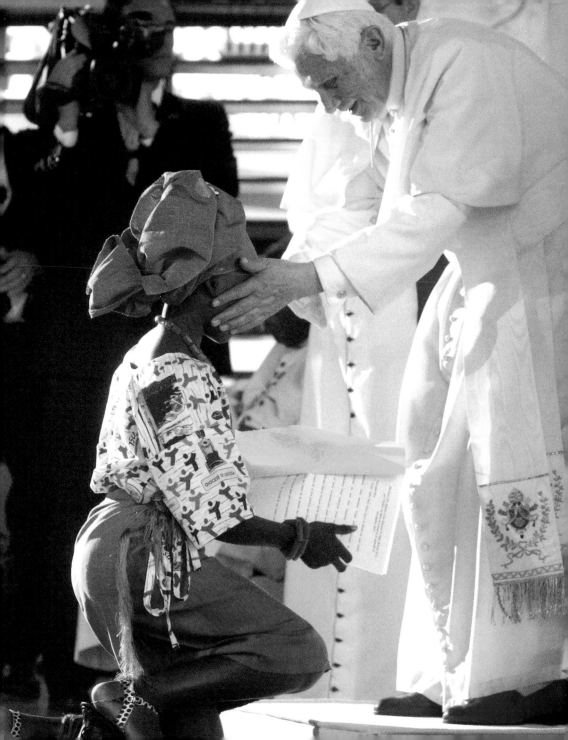

outright hostility. Benedict advanced the new evangelization, too, although his approach could be described as more intellectual than popular in its appeal. As Mass attendance and religious observance in the West continues to decline, despite the work and witness of Benedict and John Paul, this is an area where Francis will have his work cut out for him.

Many have written what they would like to see in Pope Francis, but perhaps Russell Shaw has said it best. Writing in *Our Sunday Visitor* on the eve of the election, Shaw disclosed the prayer below for the next pope.

> Let him have the charm of John XXIII, the earnestness of Paul VI, the charisma of John Paul II, the intellectual brilliance of Benedict XVI. But above all let him be a brave teacher of Catholic truth in the face of all the demands that he be something less.

Shaw's prayer is a large, even audacious one. But it is a prayer that, weeks into his pontificate, Francis seems prepared to fulfill.

The Conclave

SAINT PETER, THE FIRST POPE, was given his position by Christ Himself, but no one is entirely certain how Peter's earliest successors were chosen. Some historians believe that electing a pope was a privilege restricted to the clergy of Rome. Others believe the bishop of Rome was selected by a gathering of neighboring bishops and priests, assisted by the laity of the Church in Rome. It is also possible that the pope was chosen by popular acclamation.

With the publication in 313 of Emperor Constantine's Edict of Milan, the Church was made free from fear of persecution. But it also became exposed to political leaders who were eager to meddle in religious affairs. The Byzantine emperors in Constantinople were especially intrusive. They demanded to review the list of potential papal electors; anyone considered objectionable, the emperors would strike from the list. Furthermore, a newly elected pope could not take office until the emperors confirmed his election. This demand was especially irksome to the electors and to the pontiffs. In 649, newly elected Pope St. Martin I antagonized Emperor Constans II by failing to petition the emperor to confirm his election. Constans responded by having Martin arrested, put on trial in Constantinople for rebellion, then banished to the Crimea. Savagely beaten, half-starved, and deprived of water, the pope died of mistreatment shortly after he arrived at his place of exile.

In the ninth century, the noblemen of Rome picked the pope. In many cases this led to the pope being firmly under the thumb of Roman aristocrats. The system in place today began in 1059, when Pope Nicholas II decreed that henceforth only cardinals would elect a new pope.

Once the resignation of Benedict XVI was in force, the Church began its preparations for the conclave. The procedure has been carefully laid out over the centuries. In the absence of a pope, the camerlengo, or chamberlain, administers the properties and revenues of the Holy See. In this case, the camerlengo was Cardinal Tarsicio Bertone, Benedict's secretary of state. The morning of March 1, Bertone led a small procession to the papal apartments. He locked the doors, tied red ribbon around the door handles, poured hot wax over the ribbon and stamped it with the Vatican seal. The rooms where the pope lived would remain untouched and uninhabited until a new pope was elected.

While Bertone ran the day-to-day operations of the Church, all the preparations for the conclave were in the hands of the dean of the College of Cardinals, Cardinal Angelo Sodano, who also served as John Paul II's secretary of state. Both Bertone and Sodano are eighty-five. Pope Paul VI had decreed that cardinal electors must be under age eighty, so neither Sodano nor Bertone would vote in the conclave. Sodano, however, was in attendance—as dean it was his role to ask the new pontiff if he accepted his election.

The liturgical portion of the conclave and the installation Mass after the election was the responsibility of Benedict's master of liturgical ceremonies, Monsignor Guido Marini. Marini also served as the witness and notary during the conclave, drawing up the document attesting that the new pope had accepted his office and recording the name he had chosen.

Shortly after he was elected pope, Benedict made Guido Marini master of liturgical ceremonies. Marini and Benedict had a shared philosophy of the liturgy, and under Marini solemnity, Gregorian chant, and many other masterworks from the Church's musical patrimony returned to papal Masses.

While the cardinals were still attending general conferences and waiting for all of their confreres to arrive in Rome, a work crew assembled in the Sistine Chapel to prepare it for the conclave. They darkened the windows, installed the small stove that would burn the ballots, and set up the chairs and desks for each of the electors. The crew also raised a new floor and installed beneath it a system that would scramble any mobile phone communications. Before the cardinals entered the chapel it was swept for bugs. The cardinals were also required to surrender their smartphones and all other electronic devices.

Preparations for a new pope extended even to the Vatican Gardens. Sister Mary Ann Walsh, spokeswoman for the U.S. Conference of Catholic Bishops, wrote in the USCCB blog that as she walked by the Domus Sanctae Marthae, she noticed that the gardeners had dug up the flower bed where a floral coat of arms of Benedict XVI had been planted. The ground had been cleared and was ready for planting the floral coat of arms of the next pope.

In March 2013, the College of Cardinals numbered 207. Ninety of the cardinals were older than eighty at the time of the conclave, and were thus not eligible to vote. Of the 117 eligible cardinals, two announced that they would not be making the trip to Rome. Cardinal Julius Riyadi Darmaatmadja, S.J., archbishop emeritus of Jakarta,

Indonesia, pleaded poor health, including rapidly failing eyesight. Cardinal Keith O'Brien resigned as archbishop of St. Andrews and Edinburgh on February 18, apparently in response to accusations from three priests and one former priest that, thirty years earlier, when O'Brien was rector of a seminary, he had made sexual advances.

In the days after Benedict announced his resignation, news reports were nearly unanimous in their expectation that the cardinals would move quickly to hold a conclave and elect a new pope. It didn't quite work out like that.

By Wednesday, March 6, two of the cardinal electors still had not arrived in Rome. Cardinal Kazimierz Nycz, archbishop of Warsaw, finally arrived Wednesday afternoon, while Cardinal Jean-Baptiste Pham Minh Man, archbishop of Ho Chi Minh City, straggled in Thursday, March 7. Meanwhile, the general congregations, or meetings, of the cardinals went on as scheduled, with the cardinals discussing what they considered to be the most pressing concerns in the Church.

On the first day of the general congregations (March 4), the American cardinals held the first of what they intended to be daily press conferences. These conferences were held at the North American College, where American seminarians study for the priesthood. The American cardinals were the only group to make themselves available to the press, which led reporters from other nations to ask their cardinals why they weren't holding press briefings, too.

These press conferences bothered some of the other cardinals. But they did not surprise Father Lombardi of the Holy See's press office. "The Americans are well organized," he told a room full of journalists. "They have a good relationship with the media and so much American media . . . has come here [to cover the conclave]."

On Wednesday March 6, however, Sister Mary Ann Walsh, spokeswoman for the U.S. Conference of Catholic Bishops, informed news organizations in Rome that the College of Cardinals had decided that the Americans must suspend their daily briefings. "Concern was expressed in the general congregation about leaks of confidential proceedings," Sister Mary Ann explained. "Furthermore, all the cardinals agreed that they would no longer make themselves available to members of the press for interviews."

It appears, however, that the Americans were not the problem. The Catholic News Agency cited one of its sources as saying that it was an anonymous Italian cardinal who had divulged too much to the Italian press. The day after the American cardinals' press briefings were shut down, another scandal broke—someone was leaking complete transcripts of the general conferences to select Italian journalists. As for the cone of silence descending on the cardinals, they still spoke to reporters, albeit anonymously.

After all the cardinals finally arrived, the general congregations came to a close and the conclave to elect the pope was set to begin.

During his long papacy, Pope John Paul II made a major change to the logistics of the conclave. Traditionally, the cardinals had been housed in temporary cubicles in sealed off chambers and corridors near the Sistine Chapel. During the summer 1978 conclave that elected John Paul I, Rome was sweltering under a heat wave. The cardinals' accommodations were not air conditioned. They could not even open the windows, because they had been sealed with molten pewter—to eliminate any possibility that during the conclave a cardinal might try to communicate with the outside world. Perhaps an even bigger problem was the number of available bathrooms—only six for 120 men, some of them elderly.

John Paul II's solution was to build a hotel for the cardinals in the Vatican Gardens. The hotel, Domus Sanctae Marthae has 107 suites and twenty-three individual rooms. There are no telephones,

The Sistine Chapel

The Sistine Chapel got its name from the pope who commissioned its construction—Sixtus IV (reigned 1471-1484). At 130 feet long, 43 feet wide, and 65 feet high, the Sistine is a church-sized chapel, and for good reason: Sixtus intended to use it as his primary papal chapel, the place where he would offer Mass for the two hundred senior members of his household, as well as any visiting princes. The man he hired to build the chapel was Baccio Pontelli, a Florentine architect, about twenty-seven years old. Work began in 1477.

Pontelli's inspiration for the size of the Sistine was taken directly from Sacred Scripture: the dimensions of the chapel are exactly the same as the dimensions of the Temple of Solomon in Jerusalem. But the chapel also served a second purpose—along the top Pontelli built battlements with arrow slits for archers and channels through which boiling oil could be poured. Above the ceiling of the chapel were living quarters for soldiers. If a fortified chapel seems like and odd thing for a pope to build, bear in mind that in the fifteenth century the people of Rome had a reputation for mob violence, something Sixtus had experienced shortly after his election, when a crowd of unhappy Romans stoned him.

Over the centuries, papal conclaves have been held in various churches in various cities. The first conclave at the Vatican met in 1455 and elected Pius II. The conclave of 1484, which elected a successor to Sixtus IV, was the first held in the Sistine Chapel. Nonetheless, the cardinals never felt bound to meet in the chapel, and over the next four hundred years they met in various chapels and cham-

bers of the Vatican Palace. The tradition of the cardinals gathering in the Sistine was not firmly established until 1878. It has been the setting for conclaves ever since.

In 1996, Pope John Paul II issued a motu proprio, *Universi Dominici Gregis*, which detailed new regulations and procedures for future papal conclaves. In the document John Paul wrote, "I establish and decree by the present Constitution that the election of the Supreme Pontiff, in conformity with the prescriptions contained in the following Numbers, is to take place exclusively in the Sistine Chapel of the Apostolic Palace in the Vatican . . . where everything is conducive to an awareness of the presence of God, in whose sight each person will one day be judged." He was referring, of course, to Michelangelo's dramatic fresco of the Last Judgment, which covers the altar wall of the chapel.

TVs, or radios during the conclave, and furnishings are basic, but at least each cardinal has his own private bathroom. The support staff includes cooks, housekeepers, doctors, and nurses, as well as priests who are available to hear the cardinals' confessions. Each day during the recent conclave, shuttle buses pulled up before the hotel to transport the cardinals to the Sistine Chapel. Cardinals who decided to walk over to the palace were accompanied by guards.

After the cardinals processed into the Sistine Chapel on March 12, 2013, Giovanni Battista Re, the Senior Cardinal Elector, intoned the *Venerabilis fratres*, a prayer that invokes the Holy Spirit, the Blessed Virgin Mary, the Apostles Peter and Paul, and all the saints to guide the cardinals in electing the new pope.

After all the cardinals were within the Sistine Chapel, the choir led them in the singing of the Veni Creator Spiritus. After the Litany, the cardinals recited together the solemn oath of the electors, and then, one-by-one, they placed their hand on the Gospels and recited the key line: *"Et ego, N., Cardinalis N., spondeo, voveo, ac iuro. Sic me Deus adiuvet et haec Sancta Dei Evangelia, quae manu mea tango."* ("And I, N. Cardinal, N., promise, vow and swear. Thus, may God help me and these Holy Gospels which I touch with my hand.")

At 5:35 p.m., Roman time, after all the cardinals had taken their solemn oath to faithfully carry out their duty to elect the pope, master of ceremonies Monsignor Guido Marini, declared, *"Extra omnes"* ("Everybody out!"). The Sistine Chapel was cleared of lay people, reporters, and photographers, and the cardinals were left alone to elect a pope.

Three cardinals were chosen by lot to serve as scrutators, sometimes known as "scrutineers," during the conclave. They took their seats at a table placed before the altar, read every ballot, announced the name of each cardinal who received a vote, tabulated the votes, then burned the ballots. Two ballots were held each morning and each afternoon of the conclave. For election, a cardinal needed two-thirds of the electors' votes—in this conclave, seventy-seven votes. If the conclave had gone for three full days without anyone achieving the super-majority, the regulations would have called for a pause in the voting and a day of reflection and prayer, before voting resumed. After thirteen days of voting (and breaks for prayer every three days), if they still had not elected a pope the cardinals would put forward the names of the two top vote-getters of the last ballot, and elect a pope by a runoff vote, until one had received two-thirds of the vote. Given that this time the cardinals had a longer-than-usual period for discussion and consultation among themselves, the likelihood that the balloting would go on longer than three days was slim. Furthermore, it would have begun the new pope's reign under a pall—the public might suspect that the cardinals had been deadlocked and he was a compromise candidate.

On that first evening, the requisite votes were not achieved, and black smoke billowed from the Sistine Chapel chimney.

The cardinals retired to Domus Sanctae Marthae for the night and reconvened at the Sistine Chapel the next morning for two more rounds of voting. At 11:30 a.m., black smoke again rose from the chimney, indicating that we still did not have a pope. The cardinals then returned for two afternoon votes. There was no smoke at around 5:00 p.m., indicating that the first vote had not garnered a pope, and by 7:00 p.m., the world again turned its gaze to the small chimney atop the Sistine Chapel.

Black smoke would result in at least one more round of voting the next day; white smoke would announce to the world that the Catholic Church had a pope.

Finally, just after 7:00 p.m., Roman time, a bit of smoke puffed out from the chimney. At first, it was unclear whether the smoke was black or white, but as it began to stream out, there was no mistaking that the smoke was white.

Habemus papam! (We have a pope!)

Viva il papa! (Long live the pope!)

The crowd that had gathered at St. Peter's erupted. Residents of Rome raced toward the Vatican, and those watching around the world rejoiced. The Chair of Peter had been filled.

About an hour later, Cardinal Jean-Louis Pierre Tauran, the senior cardinal-deacon of the Vatican, announced that the Church's new shepherd on earth was Cardinal Jorge Borgoglio of Argentina, and that he would take the name Francis. Moments later, Pope Francis himself stepped out onto the balcony and, appearing somewhat shocked initially, waved to the cheering crowd. Finally, he addressed the world, saying: "You all know that the duty of the conclave was to give a bishop to Rome. It seems that my brother cardinals have gone almost to the end of the earth to get him. . . . "

Habemus papam! We have a pope! A pope from Argentina, from Latin America, from the New World. Indeed, we have a pope from the end of the earth, as Argentina extends far south, stretching out toward Antarctica. But how did a man from such a distant outpost rise to the Chair of Peter, and what does it signal for the Church moving forward?

Here is the journey of Jorge Bergoglio—Pope Francis—the pope from the end of the earth.

Born at the End of the Earth

ON AN APRIL DAY in 2005, the owner of an old brick farm-house atop Bricco Marmolato hill in the village of Portacomaro, in the northern Italian province of Asti, heard a knock on his door. Standing at his threshold was a cardinal, Jorge Bergoglio, archbishop of Buenos Aires. He was in Italy to elect a new pope—John Paul II had just died—and now that the conclave was over, he had come to see his ancestral village.

In 1854 the cardinal's grandfather, Giovanni Angelo Bergoglio, had chipped in with his three brothers to purchase the house on the hill. The current owners, the Quattrocchio Raviolas family, invited the cardinal in and gave him a tour. The house had been mod-ernized, of course, but there were still many original features that the Bergoglio brothers would have recognized—the terracotta tile floor, the stone staircase leading up to the bedrooms, the balcony with its breathtaking view of the Monferrato hills, the wine cellar. It was from this house in 1929 that the cardinal's father, twenty-one-year-old Mario Giuseppe Bergoglio, left his homeland to emi-grate to Argentina.

Life had been good in Portacomaro, but with the advent of fascism in Italy, Bergoglio felt compelled to leave. According to the records of the National Institute of Italian Statistics, that year Mario Bergoglio was one of 174,802 Italians who sought a better life somewhere else in the world.

Mario Bergoglio settled in Buenos Aires, where there was a large Italian community numbering more than 300,000. (Today, 25 million Argentines, approximately 60 percent of the population, claim some Italian descent). He found a job as a railway worker, and then he found a wife: on December 12, 1935, Mario Bergoglio married another Italian immigrant, Regina Maria Sivori. One year and five days later—December 17, 1936—the couple had a son, whom they named Jorge Mario. Two more boys and two girls would follow. To accommodate the large family, the Bergoglios bought a modest house in the barrio of Flores, a suburb of Buenos Aires.

Maria Elena, Pope Francis's only surviving sibling, recalled their childhood in Flores. Theirs was a happy and cultured household. Their father was strict, but he never raised a hand against his children. "Dad looked at us," she said, "and you preferred ten lashes to that look."

Jorge grew up to be a fun-loving, outgoing, friendly little boy. He loved tango music and another musical style native to Argentina known as *milonga*. He became (and remains) a passionate fan of the San Lorenzo de Alamgro soccer club. Pope Francis is actually a card-carrying member of the San Lorenzo fan club. According to Reuters, architect Oscar Lucchini presented then Cardinal Bergoglio with the card, and told the news service that Pope Francis "lives in a permanent state of suffering for San Lorenzo." That suffering must have eased a bit three days after Cardinal Bergoglio

was elected pope. In a match against Colon de Santa Fe, the San Lorenzo team took the field wearing a photo of Pope Francis on their shirts. San Lorenzo won.

In an interview with Richard Fausset of the *Los Angeles Times*, two friends from Jorge's school days, Ernesto Lach and Nestor Carabajo, recalled that he was a smart, popular kid. He loved pick-up games of basketball and soccer, and he collected tango records. One of Jorge's favorite stars, Ada Falcon, eventually left the stage to enter a convent.

Mario and Regina Bergoglio maintained many of the traditions of their homeland, including the festive Sunday meal that brought the whole family together for hours of good food, good wine, and lively conversation. On Saturday afternoons Regina gathered the children around the radio to listen to live broadcasts of opera. In *El Jesuita*, Cardinal Bergoglio told his biographers, Sergio Rubin and Francesca Ambrogetti, that his mother was a passionate and knowledgeable opera lover. Before the program started she would tell the children the story, and during the performance she would let them know when a major aria was about to begin. By all accounts, Bergoglio's childhood was filled with happiness, activity, and culture. He also experienced young love.

At age twelve, Jorge developed a crush on a neighbor, Amalia Damonte, who lived four houses down from the Bergoglios. He sent her a love letter, and included a drawing of a little white house with a red roof and the caption, "This is what I'll buy you when we marry." Damonte, now seventy-six years-old, came forward with her story after Bergoglio was elected pope. "These were childish things," she said of her "romance" with Jorge, "nothing more." But when her mother came upon the letter, she was not pleased. She waited for Amalia outside her school and confronted the girl. "So, you are getting letters from a boy?" Then she demanded that Amalia break off her friendship with Jorge.

At this time Jorge was a student at the Don Bosco School. He excelled in the sciences, which would lead him to major in chemistry in college. Following his years at Don Bosco, he entered a technical high school and then he went on to college where he graduated with a degree as a chemical technician.

It was revealed in a Vatican press release on Pope Francis's coat of arms that in 1953, young Jorge Bergoglio felt a call to the priesthood. The Vatican, in describing Pope Francis's motto *miserando atque eligendo* ("because he saw him through the eyes of mercy and chose him"), stated:

> [The motto] is taken from the Venerable Bede's homily on the Gospel account of the call of Matthew. It holds special meaning for the Pope because—when he was only 17-years-old, after going to confession on the Feast of St. Matthew in 1953— he perceived God's mercy in his life and felt the call to the priesthood, following the example of St. Ignatius of Loyola.

Pope Francis's sister, Maria Elena, told a reporter a story of how her brother broke the news to the family that he wanted to be a priest. One day Regina Bergoglio entered her son's room to clean. On his desk she found books of theology.

She called him, "Jorge! Come here! Didn't you tell me you were going to study medicine?"

"Yes, Mama," he answered.

"Why do you lie to me?" she asked, pointing to the theology books.

"I am not lying to you, Mama," Jorge replied. "I am going to study the medicine of the soul."

His gentleness and easy way of explaining his love for Christ was apparent even then, on the eve of his entrance into the seminary.

In 1957, when Bergoglio was twenty-one years-old, he experienced another life-changing event. He fell ill with pneumonia, and in spite of medical treatment, the disease persisted, so his doctors ran further tests. They found that in addition to the pneumonia, there were cysts on one lung. To save Bergoglio's life, surgeons removed a portion of the affected lung.

By this time Bergoglio was already studying at Immaculate Conception, the seminary for the archdiocese of Buenos Aires. Then, in March 1958, he transferred to the novitiate of the Society of Jesus.

The Society of Jesus, better known as the Jesuits, was founded on the morning of August 15, 1534, in the crypt of the Chapel of St. Denis on Montmartre in Paris. There Saint Ignatius of Loyola—a Basque nobleman and one-time soldier, gambler, and playboy—along with six friends took vows of poverty and chastity, and resolved to place themselves at the disposal of the pope to work for the good of the Catholic Church around the globe. Among

Saint Ignatius

St. Ignatius Loyola founded the Society of Jesus, better known as the Jesuits, on the morning of August 15, 1534. Today the Jesuits are the largest single religious order in the world, with approximately 19,000 priests and brothers working in 112 countries. The Jesuits have produced 42 canonized saints, 137 blesseds, and now, in Francis, their first Pope.

A Prayer of St. Ignatius Loyola
(1491-1556)

Dearest Lord, teach me to be generous. Teach me to serve Thee as Thou deservest: to give and not to count the cost; to fight and not to heed the wounds; to toil and not to seek for rest; to labor and not to seek reward, save that of knowing that I do Thy will, O God.

Offering of St. Ignatius Loyola
"Suscipe"

Take, O Lord, and receive my entire liberty, my memory, my understanding and my whole will. All that I am and all that I possess Thou hast given me: I surrender it all to Thee to be disposed of according to Thy will. Give me only Thy love and Thy grace; with these I will be rich enough and will desire nothing more.

these seven first Jesuits were Saint Francis Xavier, the future missionary to Asia, and Saint Peter Favre, who offered the Mass on the morning of the Jesuits' inception. Six years later, in 1540, Pope Paul III formally established the Society of Jesus.

At this time the Protestant Reformation was tearing Europe apart. Ignatius believed that Catholics who were well-educated in their faith and whose spiritual life was grounded in the Mass, the sacraments, and devotion to the Blessed Virgin, would be less susceptible to false doctrine. The Jesuits opened schools and colleges and seminaries that soon acquired a reputation as the best in Europe. They debated Protestant theologians, and served as theological advisors to popes, princes, and bishops. But they also worked to spread the faith. By the time of St. Ignatius's death in 1556, the Society of Jesus had one thousand members, with houses across Europe, as well as in Brazil, India, and Japan.

The Jesuits arrived in what is now Argentina in 1573. They established themselves in Cordoba, where they opened the country's first university. Later they opened another college in Buenos Aires. Thanks to the 1987 film, *The Mission*, the Jesuits are perhaps best known for their work among the Guarani tribe in Argentina, Paraguay, and southern Brazil. It was here in Argentina and other parts of South America that the Jesuits most visibly melded their missionary spirit with their unparalleled understanding of the philosophy, theology, and the tenets of the Catholic faith. It is the same combination of qualities that has been the hallmark of Pope Francis's pastoral life.

Undoer of Knots

JORGE BERGOGLIO WAS NOW A PRIEST, but he was not yet a full-fledged Jesuit. For the final part of his religious formation, his superiors sent him to the Jesuit residence at Alcala de Henares in Spain, an ancient city, founded in the first century BC by the Romans. It was also one of the first bishoprics in Spain and the birthplace of Catherine of Aragon (the ill-fated first wife of Henry VIII) and Miguel de Cervantes, the author of *Don Quixote*. And it is the home of a renowned university where, for a time, Saint Ignatius of Loyala was a student. Alcala de Henares is one of those places that makes a visitor from the New World realize just how old the Old World really is. Here Father Bergoglio completed the "tertianship;" a period at the end of a Jesuit's professional formation, when the tertian deepens his commitment to the Society of Jesus. He studied the founding documents of the Society of Jesus and made the thirty-day silent retreat based on St. Ignatius's *Spiritual Exercises*. His tertianship was completed in 1971, fifteen years after beginning his formation. On April 22, 1973, he made is final vows as a Jesuit.

By July he was back in Argentina, just in time for a meeting of all the Argentine Jesuits, and on July 31, the feast of St. Ignatius, Father Bergoglio was elected provincial—or superior—of the Society of Jesus in Argentina, a remarkably fast ascent. Almost immediately Father Bergoglio clashed with Jesuits who had adopted a pseudo-Christian Marxism and the tenets of liberation theology—ideologies that Bergoglio opposed as antithetical to the Catholic faith and the mission of the Society of Jesus. He insisted that the Jesuits remain in their customary posts as parish priests, chaplains, and teachers.

Since the 1960s, liberation theology had been gaining ground in Latin America, and many Latin American Jesuits had taken it up. Liberation theologians differ from one another in details, but in general they put forward the idea that Jesus Christ came into the world to deliver, or liberate, the poor, the oppressed, and the marginalized from economic, social, and political injustice.

Liberation theology is a theology with a political agenda. To that end, some liberation theologians used Marxist analytical methods to make the argument that the upper classes use their wealth, privilege, and access to political power to subjugate the poor. This commingling of Marxism with a supposedly Catholic theological movement—a theology that appeared to be a heartbeat away from advocating class warfare—set off alarms in the Vatican. Pope John Paul II, who had lived under a Communist regime, became an outspoken opponent of liberation theology.

The Church and the liberation theologians, however, stood on common ground when it came to their dedication to the poor and the oppressed. In his sermon at his inaugural Mass, Pope Francis said that the papacy must "open its arms to all the people of God and embrace with affection and tenderness all of humanity, in particular the poorest, the weakest, the smallest. . . . Whoever is hungry, thirsty; whoever is foreign, naked, sick, in prison." That doctrine was set forth by Jesus Christ. Yet the Marxist-flavored political activism of some liberation theologians often undermined whatever common ground they had with official Church teachings and the Magisterium, or teaching authority of the Church.

The tension between liberation theologians and the magisterium only increased when many of these theologians argued that the sins committed by individuals were virtually insignificant, that the gravest type of sinfulness is institutionalized sin, a type of sinfulness that is ingrained in a particular organization, such as the Catholic Church in Latin America. These theologians charged that the Catholic hierarchy, from the days of the conquistadors, had been in league with the secular powers to dominate and oppress the native inhabitants of the Americas. The liberation theologians had a point, but their reading of history was one-sided and their conclusions a gross misinterpretation of the mission of Christ and the Church.

Three years into his term as provincial, a military junta seized power in Argentina, and the country was plunged into what was essentially a civil war between the right-wing junta and leftist guerrillas. It became known as the Dirty War because it was clandestine. The junta's victims did not die in the open, on battlefields, but were kidnapped and taken to the Navy Mechanics School, which became a notorious detention center where many prisoners were tortured and killed. No charges were filed against the victims. There were no trials. The victims' families were not notified of their whereabouts or their fate. They simply vanished. The Argentinians call these victims—approximately thirty thousand of them—"the disappeared."

The guerrillas for their part, however, were not passive innocents.

They targeted business executives, assassinating them, bombing their homes and offices, kidnapping them and holding them for ransom. The guerrillas' acts of terrorism included bombing hotels, police stations, and, in at least one instance, a city bus.

When the Dirty War started, two Jesuit priests who were supporters of liberation theology, Father Orlando Yorio, S.J., and Father Franz Jalics, S.J., were operating a ministry to the poor in the slums of Buenos Aires. The junta regarded priests such as Yorio and Jalics as subversives. As provincial, Father Bergoglio was responsible for the safety of these two men, and he urged them to move on to a different ministry that would not attract the attention of the government. Fathers Yorio and Jalics replied that they could not abandon the poor.

Soon after this exchange between Bergoglio and the two priests, the junta arrested a guerrilla. His interrogators demanded that he reveal the names of anyone he had worked with in the past; under torture, the guerrilla gave up the names of Fathers Yorio and Jalics. Some of Bergoglio's adversaries, principally Horacio Verbitsky, who was a member of the Montoneros guerrilla organization during the Dirty War and now edits the pro-government newspaper *Pagina 12*, have accused Bergoglio of expelling the two priests from the Society of Jesus and then handing them over to the junta. But Bergoglio has many defenders, including Father Thomas Reese, former editor of the Jesuit magazine, *America*. "The junta did not get information from Bergoglio," Father Reese wrote in the *National Catholic Reporter*. "Contrary to rumor, he did not throw them out of the society and therefore remove them from the protection of the Society of Jesus."

Adolfo Pérez Esquivel, who received the Nobel Peace Prize in 1980 for his work in defense of human rights in Latin America,

gave an interview soon after Pope Francis's election to Veronica Smink of BBC News. Speaking of the Dirty War, Perez Esquivel said, "There were many bishops who were passive [and] the church hierarchy in many cases remained silent. . . . There were bishops who were complicit, but not Bergoglio." Perez Esquivel went on to praise "the silent efforts" of some leaders of the Catholic Church in Argentina, which led to the "release [of] many prisoners."

Alicia Oliveira, a former judge who was sought by the junta during the Dirty War, told a reporter with the Argentine newspaper *Perfil* that she knew Father Bergoglio and that "he had helped many people get out of the country." She told the story of a young man on the run who bore a resemblance to Bergoglio, so he gave the fugitive his identification papers and a clerical suit which enabled the young man to get to safety in Brazil.

Graciela Fernández Meijide, a human-rights activist who served on the national commission on "the disappeared," told the Argentine press, "Of all the testimony I received, never did I receive any testimony that Bergoglio was connected to the dictatorship."

After their arrest, Fathers Yorio and Jalics were interrogated for five days. Finally, the officer in charge told them, "Fathers, you were not guilty. I will ensure that you can return to the poor district." In a statement released on March 15, 2013, Father Jalics recounted what happened next. "In spite of this pledge, we were then inexplicably held in custody, blindfolded and bound, for five months." After five months in detention, the two priests were released.

In 1977, Father Yorio issued a statement in which he said that he suspected that Bergoglio was somehow linked to his arrest and the arrest of Father Jalics. But on March 20, 2013, as the accusation was swirling around the newly-elected pope, Father Jalics released his own statement: "These are the facts: Orlando Yorio and I were not reported by Father Bergoglio. . . . It is thus wrong to claim that our capture was initiated by Father Bergoglio."

What Fathers Yorio and Jalics apparently did not know is that Father Bergoglio interceded on their behalf. The commander of the Army, General Jorge Videla, had a private chaplain, and one day Father Bergoglio persuaded this priest to call in sick. Then, in place of the chaplain, Father Bergoglio said Mass for General Videla and his family. Afterward, Father Bergoglio took the opportunity to plead for clemency for the two imprisoned Jesuits. Sergio Rubin and Francesca Ambrogetti included this story in their biography of Cardinal Bergoglio, *El Jesuita*.

Soon after his release, Father Jalics left Argentina and returned to his native Germany. Today he is in his eighties, and lives at a Jesuit retreat house. Father Yorio left the priesthood. He died in 2000.

"In the face of tyranny," Father Reese wrote in the *National Catholic Reporter*, "there are those who take a prophetic stance and die martyrs. There are those who collaborate with the regime. And there are others who do what they can while keeping their heads low. . . . Those who have not lived under a dictatorship should not be quick to judge those who have, whether the dictatorship was in ancient Rome, Latin America, Africa, Nazi Germany, Communist Eastern Europe, or today's China. We should revere martyrs, but not demand every Christian be one."

Father Bergoglio's term of office as provincial of the Jesuits came to end in 1979. Angel Centeno, who served three times as Argentina's Secretary of Worship, said of Bergoglio's time as the Argentine head of the Jesuits, "He saved the Society of Jesus from collapse in the country."

Now that he was free from his responsibilities as provincial, Father Bergoglio traveled to Germany where he completed his doctoral studies. When he came home, a newspaper ran a story about Bergoglio's academic success in Germany. His grandmother, who was in the hospital at the time, showed the paper to the nuns who were caring for her. Impressed, and proud of her grandson's growing mastery of theology, she exclaimed: "He won't stop until he's pope!"

Father Bergoglio's provincial assigned him to Cordoba, the oldest Jesuit residence in Argentina, established in 1573. There he remained until the 1990s when the archbishop of Buenos Aires, Cardinal Antonio Quarracino, made Bergoglio an auxiliary bishop, then vicar general of the archdiocese, and finally coadjutor bishop with the right to succeed. At Cardinal Quarracino's death in 1998, Bishop Bergoglio did succeed him. Three years later, Pope John Paul II made Archbishop Bergoglio titular cardinal of the church of San Roberto Bellarmino in Rome—Saint Robert Bellarmine, the great Jesuit theologian.

The archbishop's residence is in Olivos, a stylish Buenos Aires suburb that is also home to Argentina's president. Instead of living

Prayer to Our Lady, Undoer of Knots

Virgin Mary, Mother of fair love, Mother who never refuses to come to the aid of a child in need, Mother whose hands never cease to serve your beloved children because they are moved by the divine love and immense mercy that exists in your heart, cast your compassionate eyes upon me and see the snarl of knots that exist in my life. You know very well how desperate I am, my pain, and how I am bound by these knots. Mary, Mother to whom God entrusted the undoing of the knots in the lives of His children, I entrust into your hands the ribbon of my life. No one, not even the Evil One himself, can take it away from your precious care. In your hands there is no knot that cannot be undone. Powerful Mother, by your grace and intercessory power with Your Son and My Liberator, Jesus, take into your hands today this knot.

(mention your petition here)

I beg you to undo it for the glory of God, once for all. You are my hope. O my Lady, you are the only consolation God gives me, the fortification of my feeble strength, the enrichment of my destitution, and, with Christ, the freedom from my chains. Hear my plea. Keep me, guide me, protect me, O safe refuge!

there, however, Bergoglio moved into a small apartment on the third floor of the chancery building; his office was on the second floor. Since the chancery is located in downtown Buenos Aires, Bergoglio ran his errands on foot or took public transportation. Claretian Father Gustavo Larrazabal, Bergoglio's long-time friend and editor of his books, said, "If in a hurry, he would take a taxi."

Father Larrazabal recalled that for his fiftieth birthday he invited Cardinal Bergoglio to Mass and to a party afterward. Larrazabal wanted the cardinal to be the principal celebrant of the Mass, but Bergoglio refused. "He said that it was my place to preside," Larrazabal told a reporter from *U.S. Catholic*, "and that he would concelebrate with my Claretian brothers and other priests present."

To describe Bergoglio's style as archbishop, Father Larrazabal recalled that Cardinal Bergoglio once told him, "As a shepherd, I allow things to happen. I allow for things to flow, provided things are within the scope of the doctrine of the church, and do not fall into heresy or absurd ideas."

"When things get out of line with the positions of the church," Larrazabal added, "he has to confront them."

Margaret Hebblethwaite, writing for the British newspaper the *Guardian*, tells the story of an unlikely friendship between Bergoglio and Clelia Luro, whom Hebblethwaite describes as "a radical feminist . . . who is about as far to the left on the ecclesial spectrum as you can go." Her husband was Jeronimo Podesta, one-time bishop of Avellaneda. Podesta believed that the documents of the Second Vatican Council called for a complete rupture with the Church's past, and he expected a dramatic reconfiguration of every aspect of Catholic life. But he was not willing to wait for the reconfiguration to happen. In 1966 he met Luro, a single mother with six children; in 1967 they began a relationship. When word of the affair reached the papal nuncio, Archbishop Umbert Mozzoni, he demanded Podesta's resignation as bishop. Podesta agreed, on the condition that Mozzoni arrange a private audience for him with Pope Paul VI. The meeting between Paul and Podesta never happened, and Podesta's case remained unresolved until 1972 when he was suspended from the clerical state. Soon thereafter Podesta and Luro married. From time to time the husband and wife said Mass together.

The Podesta case scandalized many of the faithful in Argentina, yet in 2000, when Podesta was dying, Archbishop Bergoglio visited him in the hospital—the only Argentine churchman to do so. Out of that act of compassion, a friendship sprang up between Luro and Bergoglio. She sent him notes just about every week; he called her on the phone for brief conversations. "Luro talked to me at length about her friend," Hebblethwaite writes, "of whom she has the highest opinion."

Bergoglio's relationship with Podesta and his wife offers a powerful example of his pastoral nature, of his constant desire to reach out to those on the fringes, and to try to bring them to the truth of the Church. Instead of abandoning those who have been cast off—or in this case, who have fallen away—Bergoglio always strove to bring them into the fold.

Bergoglio's concern for the abandoned and the vulnerable is expressed vividly every year on Holy Thursday in the ritual washing of feet. During his years as archbishop he washed the feet of convicts in prison, patients in a hospital, and elderly residents of a nursing home. Shortly after his election to the papacy, Pope Francis's spokesman announced that the Holy Father would offer Holy Thursday Mass at a prison for young people, where he would wash the feet of twelve youthful offenders.

In terms of liturgical life, Pope Francis brings a different style than his predecessor, while keeping firmly intact the nature and solemnity of the Holy Mass and the devotional life of the Church. While Benedict XVI often wore the splendid pre-Vatican II vestments that are among the treasures of the sacristy of St. Peter's, Pope Francis prefers the simpler style of post-Vatican II vestments. This preference has led to some concern among traditional-minded Catholics. For those who love the traditional Latin Mass, which Benedict liberated in his 2007 *motu proprio, Summorum Pontificum*, the good news is that as archbishop of Buenos Aires, Bergoglio implemented Benedict's directive within forty-eight hours, assigning a priest to say the traditional Latin Mass at the parish of San Miguel every Sunday.

Another example of Cardinal Bergoglio's devotional life—and his work as obedient servant to the Church—is his introduction to Latin America of the devotion to Our Lady, Undoer of Knots. He discovered this devotion while studying in Germany in the 1980s. The Church of St. Peter am Perlach in Augsburg enshrines a painting from about 1700 that depicts Mary untying a large knot. The inspiration for the painting and the devotion comes from the writings of St. Irenaeus of Lyon (martyred 202): "Eve, by her disobedience, tied the knot of disgrace for the human race; whereas Mary, by her obedience, undid it." Thanks to Bergoglio, veneration of Our Lady under this title has spread throughout Argentina and Brazil, where devotion is so intense that the British newspaper the *Guardian* characterized it as "a religious craze."

A Heart for the Poor

THE *NEW YORK TIMES'* first piece on Pope Francis, published within hours of his election, described him as, "A doctrinal conservative [who] has opposed liberation theology, abortion, gay marriage and the ordination of women, standing with his predecessor in holding largely traditional views."

The *Times'* assessment of Francis is correct. As archbishop of Buenos Aires he spoke out forcefully against abortion, euthanasia, child abuse and child trafficking, and prostitution. In October 2007, Cardinal Bergoglio presented to a gathering of clergy and laity the final edition of the Aparecida Document, a joint statement by the bishops of Latin America regarding the condition of the Church in their countries. In his address, Cardinal Bergoglio condemned abortion as "a death sentence" for unborn children. He said, "the most mentioned word in the Aparecida Document is 'life', because the Church is very conscious of the fact that the cheapest thing in Latin America, the thing with the lowest price, is life."

The archbishop went on to denounce the "culture of discarding" the elderly, which he charged was widespread in Argentina. "In Argentina there is clandestine euthanasia," he said. "Social services pay up to a certain point; if you pass it, 'die, you are very old.' Today, elderly people are discarded when, in reality, they are the seat of wisdom of the society." Bergoglio asserted that the right to life does not apply only to the unborn, but to human beings at every stage of life. "The right to life," he said, "means allowing people to live, to grow, to eat, to be educated, to be healed, and to be permitted to die with dignity."

On all issues related to human life, the Aparecida Document calls for "Eucharistic coherence." It states, "We should be conscious that people cannot receive Holy Communion and at the same time act or speak against the commandments, in particular when abortion, euthanasia, and other serious crimes against life and family are facilitated. This responsibility applies particularly to legislators, governors, and health professionals."

In the same speech Bergoglio denounced child trafficking. "Many [children] are made into prostitutes and exploited," he said. "And this happens here in Buenos Aires, in the great city of the south. Child prostitution is offered in some five star hotels, it is included in the entertainment menu, under the heading 'Other'." The cardinal described such abuse of children as "demographic terrorism."

The administration of Argentine president Cristina Fernandez de Kirchner, which has had many ideological clashes with Cardinal Bergoglio, issued a statement deploring Bergoglio linking child abuse, which the government considers a crime, with abortion and euthanasia, which the government considers a matter of human rights. "The diagnosis of the Church in relation to social problems in Argentina is correct," the statement read, "but to mix that with abortion and euthanasia, is at least a clear example of ideological malfeasance."

In 2010, as a bill to legalize same sex marriage was heading to the Argentine Senate, Cardinal Bergoglio sent a letter to Buenos Aires'

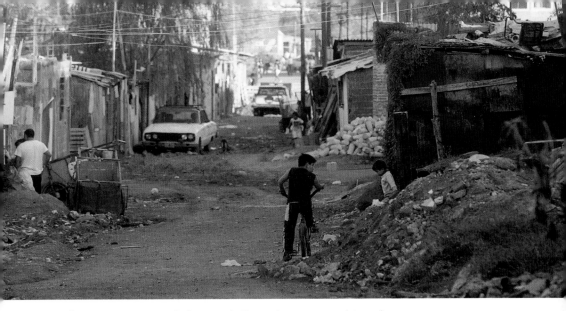

four monasteries of cloistered Carmelite nuns, asking them to pray fervently to the Holy Family that the legislation would be defeated. "Identity is at stake," he wrote, "and the survival of the family: father, mother and children . . . At stake is a direct rejection of God's law, also engraved in our hearts." The cardinal continued:

> Let us not be naïve, this is not just a simple political battle; it represents an aspiration destructive to the plan of God. This is no mere legislation (it is only the instrument) but rather a maneuver by the Father of Lies who seeks to confuse and deceive the children of God. Today the country, faced with this situation, needs the special assistance of the Holy Spirit who shines the light of truth amidst the darkness of error, we need the Divine Advocate to defend us against the enchantment of such sophistry by which they try to justify this legislation and to confuse and deceive people of good will.

In spite of the efforts of the cardinal and the fervent prayers of the

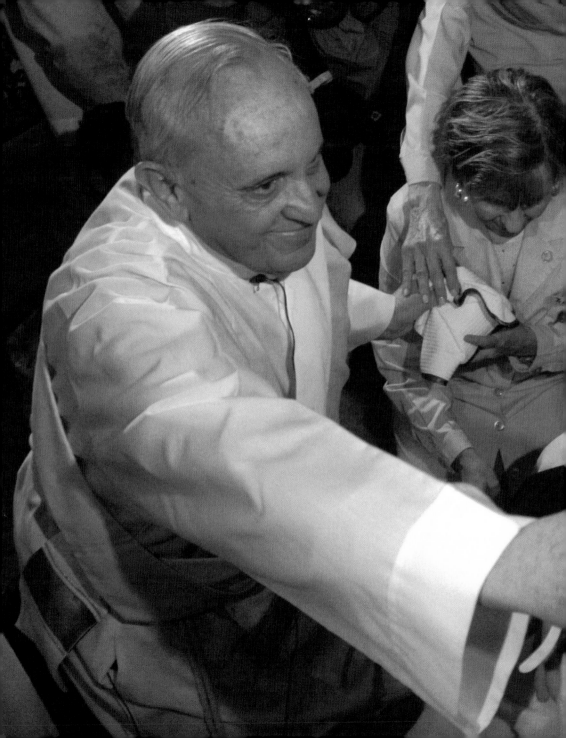

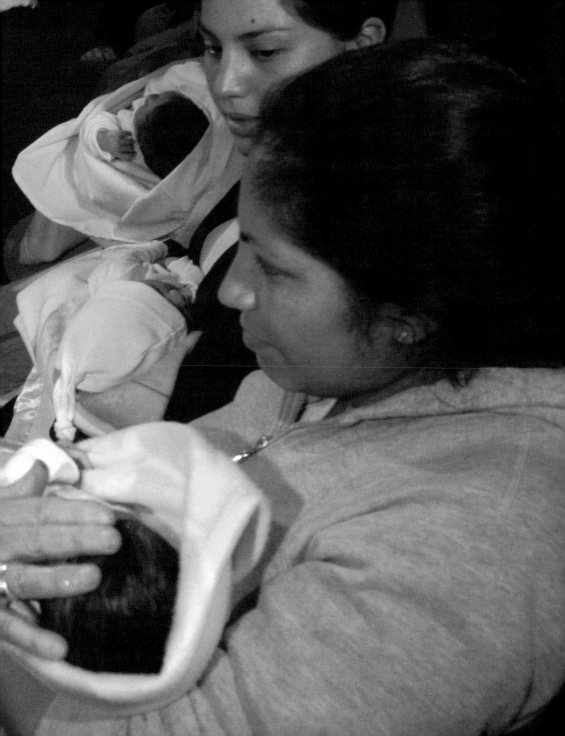

Carmelite nuns, the Senate passed the bill, making Argentina the first Latin American nation to legalize same-sex marriage.

Virtually from the beginning of their tag-team presidencies, Cardinal Bergoglio clashed with Nestor Kirchner and his wife and successor, Cristina Fernandez de Kirchner. The *Washington Post* wrote that the couple adopted a "take-no-prisoners approach to the opposition and the press." When Nestor Kirchner released documents said to show how his reforms had improved the Argentine economy and reduced the number of poor people, Bergoglio authorized a Church study, which found that the poverty rate was much higher than that in the Kirchner report. And there were other Kirchner initiatives that provoked Bergoglio: they introduced sex education to the schools, guaranteed access to free contraceptives, and granted transsexuals the right to change their identities.

May 25 is Revolution Day in Argentina, comparable to the Fourth of July in the United States. Every year, on the national holiday, a *Te Deum* is sung in the Metropolitan Cathedral of Buenos Aires and Cardinal Bergoglio would preach on the state of the nation. His critiques were carefully worded. For example, from his 2006 sermon: "Power is born of confidence, not with manipulation, intimidation or with arrogance." Oscar Agaud, a member of the Argentine congress, was quoted in the *Washington Post* as saying, "There were scraps between Bergoglio and the Kirchner governments, to the point where Nestor Kirchner even said that Bergoglio was the head of the opposition." The Kirchners stopped attending the Revolution Day *Te Deum*.

In spite of their differences, Pope Francis's first meeting with a head of state was with President Fernandez de Kirchner, who had come to Rome as the head of a nineteen-member Argentine delegation to the papal installation ceremony and Mass. She called on him at the Domus Sanctae Marthae, where he was still residing. It was a three-hour meeting that included lunch and an exchange of gifts. The president gave the pontiff a mate gourd and a straw, the traditional method of drinking Argentine tea. Then she asked Francis for a favor. As she said to reporters after the meeting, "I asked for his intervention on the question of the Malvinas [the Falkland Islands, the territory off the coast of Argentina that sparked a war between Britain and Argentina in 1982 and continues to be a point of conflict between the two countries]. I asked for his intervention to avoid problems that could emerge from the militarization of Great Britain in the south Atlantic. We want a dialogue and that's why we asked the Pope to intervene so that the dialogue is successful." Ironically, just days earlier, the residents of the Falklands had voted overwhelmingly to remain a British Overseas Territory.

Pope Francis has been described, accurately, as a champion of social justice. This description has made some Catholics feel uneasy, but it shouldn't. It is, however, an understandable reaction—since the late 1960s, at least, there have been those who believed that their advocacy for the poor and the oppressed gave them the right to pick and choose, or ignore completely, Catholic doctrine and moral teachings. They are mistaken, of course. The calendar of the saints is full of men and women who were faithful sons and daughters of the Church and tireless advocates for the poor and the marginalized—Saint Vincent de Paul, Saint Louise de Marillac, Saint Damien of Molokai, Saint Marianne Cope, and Blessed Teresa of Calcutta are just a few examples that come to mind.

The social doctrine of the Church is rooted in a fundamental concept: all human beings possess an inherent dignity because they are all children of God, and as such they deserve to be treated with respect. Saint Peter, the first pope, put it succinctly in his first epistle, "Honor all men." (1 Peter 2:17) Writing in about the year 590 in his handbook

Defender of Life

While Bergoglio has worked tirelessly for the poor, he has also been a staunch defender of the moral teachings of the Church. His pastoral ministry reminds us that, despite what some would have you believe, social justice and sound doctrine are not incompatible.

In 2010, Bergoglio spoke out against pending legislation that would make gay marriage legal in Argentina, decrying gay marriage as "a destructive attack on God's plan."

Similarly, Bergoglio has spoken out strongly against abortion and is a powerful defender of the Culture of Life. In a 2012 speech in Argentina, he said: "Abortion is never a solution . . . respect the human being small and helpless...allow birth and then be creative in the search for ways to bring [the child] to its full development."

Yet, his thoughts again turned to the poor and downtrodden, as he chastised some clergy for being overly scrupulous, instead of fostering an environment of love and compassion. Bergoglio said:

> In our ecclesiastical region there are priests who don't baptize the children of single mothers because they weren't conceived in the sanctity of marriage. These are today's hypocrites. Those who clericalize the Church. Those who separate the people of God from salvation. And this poor girl who, rather than returning the child to sender, had the courage to carry it into the world, must wander from parish to parish so that it's baptized!

In a world where being a "social justice" Catholic or being a "pro-life" Catholic often puts members of the same Church at odds, Bergoglio—Pope Francis—is a powerful witness that the two are complementary rather than mutually exclusive.

for bishops, *Pastoral Care*, Pope Saint Gregory the Great put it this way: "By nature a man is made superior to beasts, but not to other men." And Pope Leo XIII, the greatest modern exponent of the Church's social doctrine, wrote in *Rerum Novarum*, "To misuse men as though they were things in the pursuit of gain, or to value them solely for their physical powers—that is truly shameful and inhuman."

The missionaries who planted the Catholic faith in the Americas also carried with them the Church's social teachings. One of the earliest and most dramatic examples of a priest standing up for human rights in the New World occurred on the Fourth Sunday of Advent in 1511, at Concepción de la Vega on Hispaniola, an island that is today divided between Haiti and the Dominican Republic. That day, Father Antonio de Montesinos, a Dominican friar, climbed into the pulpit and addressed a congregation of Spanish colonists that included Admiral Diego Colon, son of Christopher Columbus:

> You are all in mortal sin and live and die in it, because of the cruelty and tyranny you practice among these innocent peoples. Tell me, by what right or justice do you hold these Indians in such a cruel and horrible servitude? On what authority have you waged such detestable wars against these peoples, who dwelt quietly and peacefully on their own land? Wars in which you have destroyed such infinite numbers of them by homicides and slaughters never before heard of? Why do you keep them so oppressed and exhausted, without giving them enough to eat or curing them of the sicknesses they incur from the excessive labor you give them, and they die, or rather, you kill them, in order to extract and acquire gold every day? . . . Are these not men? Do they not have rational souls? Are you not bound to love them as you love yourselves?

Don't you understand this? Don't you feel this? Why are you sleeping in such a profound lethargic slumber?

The congregation was unmoved by the friar's impassioned defense of the Indians. Instead of repenting, the leaders of the colony arranged for Father de Montesinos to be recalled to Spain.

We can hear echoes of Father de Montesinos's sermon in a sermon Cardinal Bergoglio preached in his cathedral in May 2006:

> Blind and accursed in the depths of his conscience is he who wounds that which gives us dignity. . . . How fortunate, in contrast, does one feel when justice is done, when we feel that the law was not manipulated, that justice was not just for the adepts, for those who negotiated more or had some influence to exert. How fortunate when we can feel that our country is not just for the few.

Cardinal Bergoglio returned to the theme of assaults on human dignity in a sermon on modern slavery which he preached in September 2009: "In this city of Buenos Aires, and with a lot of pain I say it, are those who 'fit' in this system and those who are 'excess,' who do not fit, the ones for whom there is no work, nor bread, nor dignity. And those who are 'excess' are material to be discarded. . . . "

The Catholic Church's view of social justice embraces the whole person, the body and the soul, life in this world and life in the world to come. An example of putting this vision of social justice into action is a Catalan Jesuit, Saint Peter Claver (1581–1654). In 1610, his superiors sent him to Cartagena in what is now Colombia. The city's magnificent harbor made it a natural center of trade between the New World and Europe. But Cartagena also welcomed ships from

Africa—approximately twelve-thousand kidnapped Africans were unloaded in Cartagena every year. They arrived half-starved, dehydrated, half-mad with fear. Some were sick, others were dying, yet whatever their condition, they were all driven into the holding pens to be sorted out and sold later.

The only white man who treated the Africans as human beings was a Jesuit, Father Alphonsus de Sandoval. Every time a slave ship arrived, he carried food, water, and medicine to the holding pens. The Africans were his parishioners, and he cared for them daily until they had all been sold off. Father de Sandoval made the newly arrived Father Claver his assistant.

In the slave pens, Peter Claver found his life's work. Like Father de Sandoval, he brought food, water, and medicine to the Africans, but he also assembled a team of interpreters who could speak one or more of the languages of Guinea, the Congo, and Angola, the lands from which most of the slaves came. Being able to communicate with them directly made it easier for Father Claver to learn what the Africans needed, and it gave him an opportunity to teach the Africans the basics of the Catholic faith. It is believed that in the forty-four years he worked in the slave pens, Father Claver baptized three hundred thousand Africans.

Most of the Africans who passed through the slave pens Father Claver would never see again, but those that were put to work in Cartagena or just outside the city he visited regularly. He continued their religious instruction, said Mass for them, and administered the sacraments.

Peter Claver's ministry was not popular in Cartagena. His superiors received complaints that Father Claver was profaning the Eucharist by giving Communion to "animals." Some citizens of Cartagena refused to set foot inside any church or chapel where Father Claver had said

Mass for slaves. Even some of his fellow Jesuits believed that Father Claver's zeal for the slaves was excessive. Nevertheless, Father Claver continued his mission of mercy.

Like St. Peter Claver, Cardinal Bergoglio understands that the Church has to "go out onto the street," to bring the gospel to the people, rather than wait for the people to come to the Church. Of course, St. Peter was evangelizing Africans who had never heard Christ's message, while Cardinal Bergoglio has been calling for the re-evangelization of Catholics who have drifted away from their faith.

In an interview with *La Stampa*'s Andrea Tornielli, Cardinal Bergoglio spoke of regarding the entire continent of South America as missionary territory, where a new generation of missionaries must re-plant the faith in a secular society that is indifferent if not openly hostile to religion. "We need to come out of ourselves and head for the periphery," the cardinal said. "We need to avoid the spiritual sickness of a Church that is self-centered: when a Church becomes like this, it grows sick. It is true that going out onto the street, as it happens to every man and every woman, implies the risk of accidents happening. But if the Church remains closed in, self-centered, it will grow old. And if I had to choose between a bumpy Church that goes out onto the streets and a sick self-centered Church, I would definitely choose the first one."

Cardinal Bergoglio, like the countless holy, selfless clerics, religious, and laypeople who built up the Church in Latin America, sees the great suffering and misery around him—and he cannot turn away from it. Addressing his brother bishops in 2007, the cardinal said, "We live in the most unequal part of the world, which has grown the most yet reduced misery the least. The unjust distribution of goods persists, creating a situation of social sin that cries out to Heaven and limits the possibilities of a fuller life for so many of our brothers."

The Bridge Builder

DURING THE GENERAL CONGREGATION, the meetings of the cardinals before the conclave, Cardinal Jorge Bergoglio delivered a brief speech on the necessity of the Catholic Church carrying the message of Christ to the entire world. "The Church is called to come out of herself and to go to the peripheries," Bergoglio said, "not only geographically, but also the existential peripheries: the mystery of sin, of pain, of injustice, of ignorance and indifference to religion, of intellectual currents, and of all misery." Then he added, "In Revelation, Jesus says that he is at the door and knocks. Obviously, the text refers to his knocking from the outside in order to enter but I think about the times in which Jesus knocks from within so that we will let him come out. A self-referential Church keeps Jesus Christ within herself and does not let him out."

As archbishop of Buenos Aires, Bergoglio set the example by reaching out to fallen away Catholics, non-Catholics, and non-believers. Since the election of Pope Francis, the media has repeatedly stated that 42 percent of the world's Catholics live in Latin America. It's well known that from the Rio Grande to the Straits of Magellan, this region is steeped in Catholicism. Cardinal Bergoglio noted this fact in his 2008 address to the bishops of Latin America. "Over the course of more than five hundred years," he said, "the Christian faith has penetrated the continent's culture and has offered a religiosity that has nourished . . . [countless] individuals." Nonetheless, that is only part of the story.

Mexico and Brazil are the world's two largest Catholic countries, but Brazil's 2010 census found that 65 percent of Brazilians identified themselves as Catholic—down dramatically from 90 percent in 1970. A study in Mexico found that between 2000 and 2010, the number of Mexicans who identified themselves as Catholic slid from 88 percent to 83—not as steep a decline as in Brazil, but the statistics are still trending downward. In Bergoglio's native Argentina, 78 percent of the population say that they are Catholic, but only 20 percent say they attend Mass regularly and follow the teachings of the Church. Pope Benedict XVI attributed the steady drop of practicing Catholics in Latin America to "secularism, hedonism, indifferentism, and the proselytism of the various sects, animist religions and new pseudo-religious expressions."

Omar Encarnacion, writing in *Foreign Affairs* magazine, reports, "In recent years, politicians from both the left and the right have defied the church in ways that would have been unthinkable only a few years ago." In Mexico, thirteen of the thirty-one states have legalized abortion, and Mexico City guarantees abortion-on-demand up to the twelfth week of pregnancy. The government of Mexico City has legalized euthanasia and same-sex marriage. Argentina has also legalized same-sex marriage, and when Cardinal Bergoglio spoke out forcefully against the measure, President Cristina Fernández de Kirchner derided him as "reminiscent of the Middle Ages and the Inquisition." In Chile, President Sebastián Piñera, a member of the Christian Democratic Party, which has long been tied to the Church, has proposed legislation that would recognize civil unions for homosexuals.

Yet increasing secularization is not the reason the Church in Latin America is losing members. "Although Catholics in the United States and Western Europe . . . are leaving the church atop a tide of secularism," writes Encarnacion, "in Latin America, Catholics are leaving because they find other religious options more appealing." He cites statistics showing that in the mid-1990s, only 4 percent of Latin Americans identified themselves as Protestant; today, Protestant denominations claim about 15 percent of all Latin Americans. The country with the largest number of Protestants is Guatemala, with 30 percent of the population.

In May 2012, during a trip to Buenos Aires, papal biographer and Catholic commentator George Weigel visited Cardinal Bergoglio. During a freewheeling conversation they got around to the state of the Catholic Church in Latin America. In a piece for the Institute on Religion and Democracy, Weigel described Bergoglio as "completely realistic and lucid about the Church's situation in Latin America. Rather than complaining about Evangelical Protestant 'sheep-rustling,' as more than a few Latin American churchmen do, the archbishop spoke with insight and conviction about the imperative of Catholicism rediscovering the power of the gospel through personal conversion to Jesus Christ."

Rather than giving in to resentment, Bergoglio offered Orthodox, Protestants, Jews, and Muslims friendship and respect. Luis Palau, a popular Protestant evangelist and a native of Argentina, who considers Pope Francis a friend, described then-Cardinal Bergoglio's approach to evangelical Protestants as one of "building bridges and showing respect, knowing the differences, but [focusing] on what we can agree on: on the divinity of Jesus, his virgin birth, his resurrection, the second coming."

Palau recalled that Bergoglio always asked people to pray for him (just as he did on the night of his election). Juan Pablo Bongarrá, president of the Argentine Bible Society, confirmed Palau's statement. "Whenever you talk to him," Bongarra said, "the conversation ends with a request: 'Pastor, pray for me.'" Then Bongarrá told a story. Once, Cardinal Bergoglio came to a charismatic evangelical worship service. He was invited to address the congregation of about six thousand people, and he concluded with the now-familiar request, "Pastors, pray for me." Then the cardinal knelt and the pastors laid hands upon him and prayed.

Bergoglio encouraged Catholic organizations to partner with evangelical organizations to resist the increasing secularization of Argentine society, and they worked together to oppose same-sex marriage. "We evangelical leaders that know him are very happy with his election," Bongarrá said. "Bergoglio is a great man of God. We have had a good relationship with him for many years. We think that a new time is coming for the Catholic Church, because our brother wants to promote evangelism."

In terms of theology, history, liturgy, the sacraments, and devotional

The Church and Other Religions

Jorge Bergoglio, throughout his pastoral ministry, has endeavored to foster ecumenism and interreligious dialogue. He has prayed with Orthodox leaders and evangelical pastors. And he has reached out to Jewish and Muslim leaders, even publishing a book of conversations he had with Rabbi Abraham Skorka called *Sobre el Cielo y la Tierra (On Heaven and Earth)*.

His outreach is inspiring, but not surprising. It is grounded in Church teaching, especially as found in two documents of the Second Vatican Council: *Unitatis Redintegratio* and *Nostra Aetate*.

Unitatis Redintegratio sets forth how the Catholic Church should relate to other Christian bodies. The document affirms the constant teaching that the Catholic Church is the one Church founded by Christ, and is in fact the Body of Christ on earth. Yet other Christians are part of this Body too, by virtue of their baptism, though imperfectly. As the decree says, "all who have been justified by faith in Baptism are members of Christ's body, and have a right to be called Christian, and so are correctly accepted as brothers by the children of the Catholic Church."

Non-Christians are not related to the Catholic Church in the same way. But there is a deep connection nonetheless. All men and women are made in the image and likeness of God, and God loves and desires all to be saved. Thus Pope Paul VI writes in *Nostra Aetate*:

> We cannot truly call on God, the Father of all, if we refuse to treat in a brotherly way any man, created as he is in the image of God. Man's relation to God the Father and his relation to

men his brothers are so linked together that Scripture says: "He who does not love does not know God" (1 John 4:8).

No foundation therefore remains for any theory or practice that leads to discrimination between man and man or people and people, so far as their human dignity and the rights flowing from it are concerned.

The Church reproves, as foreign to the mind of Christ, any discrimination against men or harassment of them because of their race, color, condition of life, or religion. On the contrary, following in the footsteps of the holy Apostles Peter and Paul, this sacred synod ardently implores the Christian faithful to "maintain good fellowship among the nations" (1 Peter 2:12), and, if possible, to live for their part in peace with all men, so that they may truly be sons of the Father who is in heaven.

life, the Catholic Church is closest to the Orthodox Churches. The Orthodox went into schism in 1056, but since then, time and again, there have been efforts to heal the breach. In the twentieth century, Paul VI and John Paul II were especially keen to find some way to end the schism and reunite the two churches, and it appears that Pope Francis will continue these efforts. As archbishop of Buenos Aires he represented the interests of Argentine Orthodox Christians in their dealings with the national government, and he was a friend of Antoni Sevruk, rector of the Russian Orthodox Church of Saint Catherine the Great Martyr, a short walk from St. Peter's Basilica. The surest sign of friendly feelings between the new pope and the Orthodox was the presence of the Ecumenical Patriarch Bartholomew at the Installation Mass. It was the first time in history that a Patriarch of Constantinople, the head of the Orthodox world, had attended the enthronement of a Roman pontiff.

On July 18, 1994, an unknown person or persons parked a Renault van in front of the Argentine Israelite Mutual Association building in Buenos Aires and detonated 610 pounds of explosives. The blast virtually destroyed the building, killing eighty-five people and wounding more than three hundred. The majority of the victims were Jews. The bombing was the worst in the history of Argentina, yet it took ten years before charges were filed and the suspects were brought to trial. The case degenerated into a travesty of cover-ups, irregularities, and judicial incompetence so serious that the presiding judge was impeached. In the aftermath of the bungled trial, Cardinal Bergoglio was the first public figure to call for justice—an act which endeared him to the Jewish community of Argentina.

Before the botched trial, Bergoglio and Argentine Jews forged a close relationship. In the early 2000s, the cardinal and Israel Singer, former head of the World Jewish Congress, started a joint Catholic-

Jewish organization called Tzedaka to distribute aid to poor Catholics and Jews. In 2012, Cardinal Bergoglio invited Jews and Christians to mark the seventy-fourth anniversary of Kristallnacht, the Nazis' attack on Jewish synagogues, businesses, and homes in Germany and Austria, with an ecumenical prayer service in the Metropolitan Cathedral. And in 2007, the cardinal attended Rosh Hashanah services at a Buenos Aires synagogue. Addressing the congregation, he said that he had come to examine his heart, "like a pilgrim, together with you, my elder brothers."

In 2011, Cardinal Bergoglio and Rabbi Abraham Skorka published a book of their conversations on a host of topics, religious and secular. In the book, entitled *Sobre el cielo y la tierra*, Bergoglio defines his concept of interfaith dialogue:

> Dialogue is born from an attitude of respect for the other person, from a conviction that the other person has something good to say. It assumes that there is room in the heart for the person's point of view, opinion, and proposal. To dialogue entails a cordial reception, not a prior condemnation. In order to dialogue it is necessary to know how to lower the defenses, open the doors of the house, and offer human warmth.

Bergoglio also worked hard to build relationships with the leaders of Islam: a task that, in his view, was hampered early in Pope Benedict XVI's papacy. In 2005, Benedict traveled to Regensburg, Germany, to deliver a lecture at the university. During his address, he referred to a debate in 1391 between a Muslim scholar and the Byzantine emperor, Manuel II Paleologus, and he quoted the emperor as saying that if one examined the career of Mohammed, one would find "things only evil and inhuman, such as his command to spread by the sword the faith he preached." Benedict went on to distance himself from the Emperor and condemned violence of any kind, but the quotation outraged Muslims across the globe. At the time, Cardinal Bergoglio criticized Benedict for quoting something so inflammatory, which he felt had served only to damage the relationship with Islam that Pope John Paul II had forged.

For his part, Bergoglio began a nearly decade-long effort to foster open, respectful dialogue between Muslims and Christians, which Dr. Sumer Noufouri, Secretary General of the Islamic Center of the Argentine Republic, praised as "really significant in the history of monotheistic relations in Argentina." After Cardinal Bergoglio's election as pope, Ahmed el-Tayeb, Grand Imam of Al-Azhar and president of Egypt's prestigious Al-Azhar University sent his congratulations to Pope Francis. It was Imam el-Tayeb's first contact with the Vatican in more than a year—the university had broken off all contact with Rome after Pope Benedict, in the wake of a church bombing in Alexandria, had called upon the Egyptian government to provide greater protection for its Coptic Christian citizens.

Already in his brief papacy, Pope Francis has begun to reopen those channels of interreligious dialogue. Three days after his installation as pope, Francis met with the ambassadors from the 180 countries assigned to the Holy See. He reminded his audience that his title, "pontiff" comes from the Latin term for "bridge builder." He went on to say, "My wish is that the dialogue between us should help to build bridges connecting all people, in such a way that everyone can see in the other not an enemy, not a rival, but a brother or sister to be welcomed and embraced."

Go to the Outskirts

EVERY MAN WHO IS ELECTED POPE brings his own priorities and personality to the office. John Paul II was the universal pastor, traveling the world to visit his flock. Benedict XVI was the brilliant teacher, presenting the ancient truths of the faith and the timeless traditions of the Church to the modern world in a way that it could understand. It's early in the papacy of Pope Francis, but it appears that his inspiration comes from the most humble of the pope's many titles—servant of the servants of God.

Pope Francis has something significant in common with the saint of Assisi whose name he took—he is not comfortable with pomp. When he addresses an audience or a congregation he sits in an upholstered white chair. It is a very nice chair, but it is not a throne. He continues to wear the simple pectoral cross he wore as archbishop of Buenos Aires rather than replacing it with any of the beautiful gold crosses and crucifixes that are part of the papal wardrobe. He has chosen to live at the Domus Sanctae Marthae, the hotel where he and his fellow cardinals stayed during the conclave, leaving the Apostolic Palace empty. He has a suite of two or three rooms. He takes his meals in the dining room with the other residents and guests of the hotel. Every morning at seven o'clock he says Mass in the hotel's chapel before a congregation of Vatican bureaucrats and the hotel's cooks and housekeepers. He does use the office at the Apostolic Palace, which is more convenient for working with Vatican officials, and he does receive visiting dignitaries in the splendid Clementine Hall, which is proper—there are times when a little formality is necessary.

The papacy is a sacred office, so there is a degree of grandeur and majesty to being the Vicar of Jesus Christ, the Successor to St. Peter, the shepherd of approximately 1.2 billion souls. But grandeur and majesty can get in the way when trying to connect with people, and, throughout his life as a priest, Francis has tried to make connections. The Jesuits, it should be remembered, have always been at heart a missionary order, and a successful missionary goes to people who need him: he lives with them and like them; he listens to their joys and troubles; he offers them consolation—the human kind first and the supernatural variety a little later when they are ready to hear it. To get to that point of trust and connection when a soul feels drawn to God is the goal of every evangelist.

The world has seen how Francis reaches out to people, how he wants to be among them and part of them: preferring to refer to himself simply as "bishop of Rome" rather than pope; asking for the crowd's prayers before giving them his first blessing; taking the bus back to the Domus Sanctae Marthae with the cardinals who had just elected him; greeting the people after his first Mass at Santa Anna, like a common parish priest; and living at the Vatican hotel, where he will be among ordinary working folks every day, rather than living in the splendid isolation of the Apostolic Palace.

In his early audiences he has made a point to be among the people.

He greets the crowd from an open Jeep rather than from inside the bullet-proof popemobile (his security team may yet convince him that the fortified vehicle is more prudent) and he displays a sincere and tender love for his flock. Already he has reached out to the people, and held children and the unfortunate in his arms. He has shown himself to be a loving father to his children in the Church. And he has encouraged Catholics to go out into the world with the same love that he has extended to them.

Francis is setting the example, and urging his fellow Catholics to get out there and share their faith as he does. At his first general audience he encouraged the crowd to "move beyond a dull or mechanical way of living our faith, and instead open the doors of our hearts, our lives, our parishes, our movements or associations, going out in search of others so as to bring them the light and the joy of our faith in Christ."

Inherent in this mission is the willingness to serve. On Holy Thursday, Pope Francis said Mass for the inmates of del Marmo, a prison for juvenile offenders. During the Mass, he removed his

chasuble, took a basin and a towel, and washed the feet of twelve young offenders—ten young men and two young women. The ritual washing imitates what Christ did at the beginning of the Last Supper, when he washed the feet of the twelve apostles. It is a lesson in humility, but also of service, as Jesus explained to his apostles: "If I then, your Lord and Teacher, have washed your feet, you also ought to wash one another's feet." (John 13:14)

As Pope Francis explained to his congregation of inmates:

> This is a symbol, it is a sign—washing your feet means I am at your service. And we are too, among each other, but we don't have to wash each other's feet each day. So what does this mean? That we have to help each other. . . . This is what Jesus teaches us. This is what I do. And I do it with my heart. I do this with my heart because it is my duty, as a priest and bishop I must be at your service. But it is a duty that comes from my heart and a duty I love. I love doing it because this is what the Lord has taught me. But you too must help us and help each other, always.

It was not just laypeople, represented by the young offenders, that Pope Francis challenged on Holy Thursday, 2013. That morning, at the Chrism Mass he celebrated in St. Peter's Basilica, he addressed the hundreds of priests in the congregation: "Go out . . . to the outskirts where there is suffering, bloodshed, blindness that longs for sight, and prisoners in thrall to many evil masters . . . go out and give [yourselves] and the Gospel to others."

Pope Francis's emphasis on outreach and selfless service could revitalize a hope that both John Paul II and Benedict XVI shared— the re-evangelization of the West. As archbishop of Buenos Aires

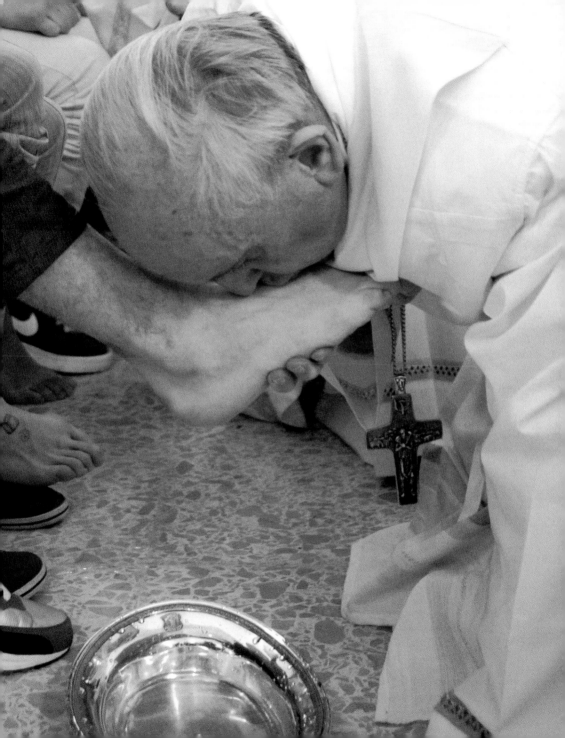

Who Is Saint Francis of Assisi?

The Italians called Saint Francis of Assisi, *il Poverello*, the Little Poor Man. In fact, he was not poor—his family was well-to-do, a member of medieval Italy's rising and soon-to-be-wealthy merchant class. But Francis turned his back on his family's money to become as poor as the Lord he loved and desired to imitate.

Francis carried the message of the gospel to the places where ordinary people gathered—the piazzas, the marketplaces, and the fields. Francis and the men who joined him—in time they would be known as Franciscans—were at the forefront of a movement to re-evangelize the Catholic world, and it was in direct response to a vision Francis had of the crucified Christ who said to him, "Francis! Rebuild my Church which as you can see has fallen into ruins."

The Franciscans were admired for the austerity and holiness of their lives, and because these friars were accessible. Living among the people made it easier for them to offer religious counsel, to hear confessions, and to foster devotions to the Passion of Christ, the Infant Jesus, the Blessed Sacrament, and the Blessed Virgin—all especially dear to St. Francis's heart.

It has been said that no saint imitated Jesus Christ more closely than St. Francis, and that resemblance became especially profound in 1224. That summer Francis traveled with a few companions to an isolated cave on La Verna, a rugged mountain north of Arezzo. On or near the Feast of the Exaltation of the Holy Cross, September 14, Francis had a vision of a seraph. The angel's six wings burned like fire and its hands and feet were fixed to a cross. When Francis came out of his ecstasy he found on his hands, feet, and side the marks of Christ's passion. This is the first recorded instance of the stigmata.

and now as pope, Francis has shown himself committed to regaining the souls the Church has lost.

At the same time, Francis has spent a lifetime working with the poor and the unwanted. He took the name Francis in honor of St. Francis of Assisi who, to more closely imitate Jesus, voluntarily became destitute, with no place he could call home and no idea where his next meal was coming from. In his address to the ambassadors to the Holy See, the pope spoke of St. Francis's love for the poor. Then he exclaimed, "How many poor people there still are in the world!" And he mentioned that it has always been the work of the Church to assist the helpless. "I think in many of your countries you can attest to the generous activity of Christians who dedicate themselves to helping the sick, orphans, the homeless and all the marginalized, thus striving to make society more humane and more just," he said.

"But there is another form of poverty," Pope Francis continued. "It is the spiritual poverty of our time, which afflicts the so-called richer countries particularly seriously." That spiritual poverty, Francis said, was the fruit of the "tyranny of relativism, which makes everyone his own criterion and endangers the coexistence of peoples."

In using the phrase, "tyranny of relativism," Pope Francis echoed a sentiment of his predecessor, Pope Benedict. In 2005, in his homily to the cardinals who would elect him pope, Cardinal Joseph Ratzinger warned, "We are moving toward a dictatorship of relativism which does not recognize anything as for certain and which has as its highest goal one's own ego and one's own desires."

The danger of relativism is something Ratzinger had been thinking about for some time. In his book, *Without Roots*, he wrote:

The more relativism becomes the generally accepted way of thinking, the more it tends toward intolerance. Political correctness . . . seeks to establish the domain of a single way of thinking and speaking. Its relativism creates the illusion that it has reached greater heights than the loftiest philosophical achievements of the past. It presents itself as the only way to think and speak—if, that is, one wishes to stay in fashion.

It appears that Pope Francis shares Benedict's apprehension about the power of relativism to distort the truth and mislead souls.

Pope Francis has shown during the early days of his papacy that he intends to combat the struggles going on in the world—be it poverty, relativism, or secularism—as well as the struggles within the Church, with love, prayer, and a deep devotion to the Blessed Mother.

Already he has consecrated his papacy to Our Lady with his visit to Saint Mary Major and his time of prayer in front of the ancient icon, the *Salus Populi Romani*, that is enshrined there. Furthermore, in one of his first strolls through the Vatican grounds, Francis stopped to pray at the shrine to the Madonna in the papal gardens.

At this writing, Francis has been pope for only a short time. The media and the general public are still gushing over the novelty of a pope from Argentina, a pope who wears black shoes instead of red, a pope who lives in a smallish hotel suite instead of the pope's apartment in the Apostolic Palace, a pope who urges us to love and help one another, especially those who are most in need of our assistance. All interesting details that tell us something about the man the cardinals brought to us from the end of the earth. But no matter what color shoes he wears, Francis is the pope, the successor of St. Peter, the man with the weight of the world—both Catholic and non-Catholic—upon his shoulders and upon his conscience.

It is a daunting responsibility, one that exhausted Benedict XVI, and probably many popes before him. The papacy will certainly take its toll on Pope Francis as well, but in that regard he has been blessed with a great helper and model in Pope Emeritus Benedict XVI. Ten days after he became pope, Francis took the papal helicopter to Castel Gandolfo to visit the resting Benedict. The two talked and prayed together in the first meeting of two popes since 1294.

In keeping with his early theme of devotion to Our Lady, Pope Francis presented Benedict with an icon of Our Lady and Christ—"Our Lady of Humility"—that the Russian Orthodox delegation had presented him days before at his installation.

The two had spoken on the phone at least twice before the historic visit, and when they came together face-to-face, Francis commented, "We're brothers." For his part, Benedict reiterated his full obedience to Francis and promised to pray for his successor. After the meeting, Vatican spokesman, Father Federico Lombardi, told reporters:

> The retired pope had already expressed his unconditional reverence and obedience to his successor at his farewell meeting with the cardinals, February 28, and certainly in this meeting—which was a moment of profound and elevated communion—he will have had the opportunity to renew this act of reverence and obedience to his successor.

As Francis began to settle into his role as pope after a whirlwind ten days, this meeting between two popes served as a beautiful reminder of the constancy and stability of the Church in a world that each day becomes more tumultuous. Amid a raging sea of secularism and relativism, and a growing swell of anti-Christian sentiment, the

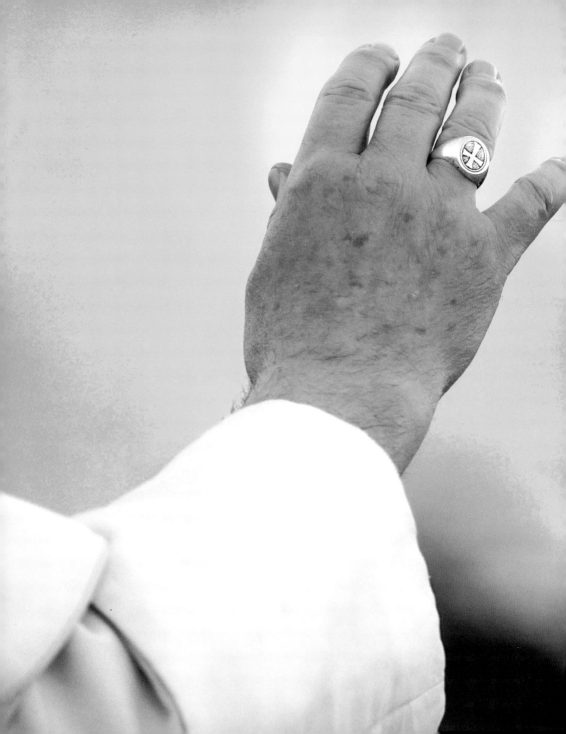

Church stands firm upon that unyielding rock, given to the Church by Christ himself.

Despite all the uncertainty and anxiety that followed Benedict XVI's resignation, and the anticipation of what lies ahead in the reign of Pope Francis, one thing is certain: the Catholic Church, instituted and safeguarded by Christ, will endure.

That fact was made clear when Benedict XVI greeted Pope Francis with a spirit of obedience and a reverent, loving embrace. Francis will continue—in his own way and with his own unique talents and gifts—the mission that Benedict took up from John Paul II, and so on back through the years to Peter, and to Christ himself: the mission to bring souls to heaven and to restore all things in Christ.

Viva il papa!

MISSA PRO ECCLESIA
WITH THE CARDINAL ELECTORS

Pope Francis's First Homily: March 14, 2013, Sistine Chapel

IN THESE THREE READINGS, I see a common element: that of movement. In the first reading, it is the movement of a journey; in the second reading, the movement of building the Church; in the third, in the Gospel, the movement involved in professing the faith. Journeying, building, professing.

Journeying. "O house of Jacob, come, let us walk in the light of the Lord" (Is 2:5). This is the first thing that God said to Abraham: Walk in my presence and live blamelessly. Journeying: our life is a journey, and when we stop moving, things go wrong. Always journeying, in the presence of the Lord, in the light of the Lord, seeking to live with the blamelessness that God asked of Abraham in his promise.

Building. Building the Church. We speak of stones: stones are solid; but living stones, stones anointed by the Holy Spirit. Building the Church, the Bride of Christ, on the cornerstone that is the Lord himself. This is another kind of movement in our lives: building.

Thirdly, professing. We can walk as much as we want, we can build many things, but if we do not profess Jesus Christ, things go wrong. We may become a charitable NGO, but not the Church, the Bride of the Lord. When we are not walking, we stop moving. When we are not building on the stones, what happens? The same thing that happens to children on the beach when they build sandcastles: everything is swept away, there is no solidity. When we do not profess Jesus Christ, the saying of Léon Bloy comes to mind: "Anyone who does not pray to the Lord prays to the devil." When we do not profess Jesus Christ, we profess the worldliness of the devil, a demonic worldliness.

Journeying, building, professing. But things are not so straightforward, because in journeying, building, professing, there can sometimes be jolts, movements that are not properly part of the journey: movements that pull us back.

This Gospel continues with a situation of a particular kind. The same Peter who professed Jesus Christ, now says to him: You are the Christ, the Son of the living God. I will follow you, but let us not speak of the Cross. That has nothing to do with it. I will follow you on other terms, but without the Cross. When we journey without the Cross, when we build without the Cross, when we profess Christ without the Cross, we are not disciples of the Lord, we are worldly: we may be bishops, priests, cardinals, popes, but not disciples of the Lord.

My wish is that all of us, after these days of grace, will have the courage, yes, the courage, to walk in the presence of the Lord, with the Lord's Cross; to build the Church on the Lord's blood which was poured out on the Cross; and to profess the one glory: Christ crucified. And in this way, the Church will go forward.

My prayer for all of us is that the Holy Spirit, through the intercession of the Blessed Virgin Mary, our Mother, will grant us this grace: to walk, to build, to profess Jesus Christ crucified. Amen.

INSTALLATION MASS
IMPOSITION OF THE PALLIUM AND BESTOWAL OF THE FISHERMAN'S RING FOR THE BEGINNING OF THE PETRINE MINISTRY OF THE BISHOP OF ROME

Pope Francis's homily at his Installation Mass, March 19, 2013, Saint Peter's Square on the Solemnity of Saint Joseph

DEAR BROTHERS AND SISTERS,

I thank the Lord that I can celebrate this Holy Mass for the inauguration of my Petrine ministry on the solemnity of Saint Joseph, the spouse of the Virgin Mary and the patron of the universal Church. It is a significant coincidence, and it is also the name-day of my venerable predecessor: we are close to him with our prayers, full of affection and gratitude.

I offer a warm greeting to my brother cardinals and bishops, the priests, deacons, men and women religious, and all the lay faithful. I thank the representatives of the other Churches and ecclesial Communities, as well as the representatives of the Jewish community and the other religious communities, for their presence. My cordial greetings go to the Heads of State and Government, the members of the official Delegations from many countries throughout the world, and the Diplomatic Corps.

In the Gospel we heard that "Joseph did as the angel of the Lord commanded him and took Mary as his wife" (*Mt* 1:24). These words already point to the mission which God entrusts to Joseph: he is to be the *custos*, the protector. The protector of whom? Of Mary and Jesus; but this protection is then extended to the Church, as Blessed John Paul II pointed out: "Just as Saint Joseph took loving care of Mary and gladly dedicated himself to Jesus Christ's upbringing, he likewise watches over and protects Christ's Mystical Body, the Church, of which the Virgin Mary is the exemplar and model" (*Redemptoris Custos*, 1).

How does Joseph exercise his role as protector? Discreetly, humbly and silently, but with an unfailing presence and utter fidelity, even when he finds it hard to understand. From the time of his betrothal to Mary until the finding of the twelve-year-old Jesus in the Temple of Jerusalem, he is there at every moment with loving care. As the spouse of Mary, he is at her side in good times and bad, on the journey to Bethlehem for the census and in the anxious and joyful hours when she gave birth; amid the drama of the flight into Egypt and during the frantic search for their child in the Temple; and later in the day-to-day life of the home of Nazareth, in the workshop where he taught his trade to Jesus.

How does Joseph respond to his calling to be the protector of Mary, Jesus and the Church? By being constantly attentive to God, open to the signs of God's presence and receptive to God's plans, and not simply to his own. This is what God asked of David, as we heard in the first reading. God does not want a house built by men, but faithfulness to his word, to his plan. It is God himself who builds the house, but from living stones sealed by his Spirit. Joseph is a "protector" because he is able to hear God's voice and be guided by his will; and for this reason he is all the more sensitive to the persons

entrusted to his safekeeping. He can look at things realistically, he is in touch with his surroundings, he can make truly wise decisions. In him, dear friends, we learn how to respond to God's call, readily and willingly, but we also see the core of the Christian vocation, which is Christ! Let us protect Christ in our lives, so that we can protect others, so that we can protect creation!

The vocation of being a "protector", however, is not just something involving us Christians alone; it also has a prior dimension which is simply human, involving everyone. It means protecting all creation, the beauty of the created world, as the Book of Genesis tells us and as Saint Francis of Assisi showed us. It means respecting each of God's creatures and respecting the environment in which we live. It means protecting people, showing loving concern for each and every person, especially children, the elderly, those in need, who are often the last we think about. It means caring for one another in our families: husbands and wives first protect one another, and then, as parents, they care for their children, and children themselves, in time, protect their parents. It means building sincere friendships in which we protect one another in trust, respect, and goodness. In the end, everything has been entrusted to our protection, and all of us are responsible for it. Be protectors of God's gifts!

Whenever human beings fail to live up to this responsibility, whenever we fail to care for creation and for our brothers and sisters, the way is opened to destruction and hearts are hardened. Tragically, in every period of history there are "Herods" who plot death, wreak havoc, and mar the countenance of men and women.

Please, I would like to ask all those who have positions of responsibility in economic, political and social life, and all men and women of goodwill: let us be "protectors" of creation, protectors of God's plan inscribed in nature, protectors of one another and of the environment. Let us not allow omens of destruction and death to accompany the advance of this world! But to be "protectors", we also have to keep watch over ourselves! Let us not forget that hatred, envy and pride defile our lives! Being protectors, then, also means keeping watch over our emotions, over our hearts, because they are the seat of good and evil intentions: intentions that build up and tear down! We must not be afraid of goodness or even tenderness!

Here I would add one more thing: caring, protecting, demands goodness, it calls for a certain tenderness. In the Gospels, Saint Joseph appears as a strong and courageous man, a working man, yet in his heart we see great tenderness, which is not the virtue of the weak but rather a sign of strength of spirit and a capacity for concern, for compassion, for genuine openness to others, for love. We must not be afraid of goodness, of tenderness!

Today, together with the feast of Saint Joseph, we are celebrating the beginning of the ministry of the new Bishop of Rome, the Successor of Peter, which also involves a certain power. Certainly,

Jesus Christ conferred power upon Peter, but what sort of power was it? Jesus' three questions to Peter about love are followed by three commands: feed my lambs, feed my sheep. Let us never forget that authentic power is service, and that the Pope too, when exercising power, must enter ever more fully into that service which has its radiant culmination on the Cross. He must be inspired by the lowly, concrete and faithful service which marked Saint Joseph and, like him, he must open his arms to protect all of God's people and embrace with tender affection the whole of humanity, especially the poorest, the weakest, the least important, those whom Matthew lists in the final judgment on love: the hungry, the thirsty, the stranger, the naked, the sick and those in prison (cf. *Mt* 25:31-46). Only those who serve with love are able to protect!

In the second reading, Saint Paul speaks of Abraham, who, "hoping against hope, believed" (*Rom* 4:18). Hoping against hope! Today too, amid so much darkness, we need to see the light of hope and to be men and women who bring hope to others. To protect creation, to protect every man and every woman, to look upon them with tenderness and love, is to open up a horizon of hope; it is to let a shaft of light break through the heavy clouds; it is to bring the warmth of hope! For believers, for us Christians, like Abraham, like Saint Joseph, the hope that we bring is set against the horizon of God, which has opened up before us in Christ. It is a hope built on the rock which is God.

To protect Jesus with Mary, to protect the whole of creation, to protect each person, especially the poorest, to protect ourselves: this is a service that the Bishop of Rome is called to carry out, yet one to which all of us are called, so that the star of hope will shine brightly. Let us protect with love all that God has given us!

I implore the intercession of the Virgin Mary, Saint Joseph, Saints Peter and Paul, and Saint Francis, that the Holy Spirit may accompany my ministry, and I ask all of you to pray for me! Amen.

BIBLIOGRAPHY

Aguinaco, Carmen. "An inside look at Pope Francis." U.S. Catholic, March 25, 2013. http://www.uscatholic.org/articles/201303/inside-look-pope-francis-27083#?utm_source=March+26%2C+2013&utm_campaign=ebulletin+March+26%2C+2013&utm_medium=email (accessed March 27, 2013)

Aguirre, Estefania and David Uebbing. "College of Cardinals imposes media silence after breach." Catholic News Agency, March 6, 2013.

Allen, John L. *Conclave: The Politics, Personalities, and Process of the Next Papal Election* (Revised and Updated). Doubleday, 2004.

Allen, John L. "Picking a pope a contest among four camps." *National Catholic Reporter*, March 1, 2013.

Arkell, Harriet. "You still haven't got a prayer, Mrs. Kirchner: Argentina's president flies to Rome to ask compatriot Pope Francis to intervene in Falklands row." *Daily Mail*, March 18, 2013.

Bellitto, Christopher. *101 Questions & Answers on Popes and the Papacy*. Paulist Press, 2008.

Bellos, Alex. "Virgin painting ties Brazilians in knots." the *Guardian*, December 23, 2001.

Benedict XVI. "Faith, Reason and the University: Memories and Reflections." http://www.vatican.va/holy_father/benedict_xvi/speeches/2006/september/documents/hf_ben-xvi_spe_20060912_university-regensburg_en.html (accessed March 28, 2013)

Bergoglio, Jorge Mario. "Evangelizing implies Apostolic zeal." http://en.radiovaticana.va/m_articolo.asp?c=677269 (accessed March 28, 2013)

The Catholic Encyclopedia (www.newadvent.org)

"Catholic faith up 33% in Africa, 16% in Asia." *USA Today*, April 27, 2010.

Catholic Online. "New Pope: Who is this man named Bergoglio?" March 14, 2013. http://www.catholic.org/hf/faith/story.php?id=50111 (accessed March 18, 2013)

Chambers, D.S. "Papal Conclaves and Prophetic Mystery in the Sistine Chapel." *Journal of Warburg and Courtauld Institutes*, Vol. 41, (1978), pp. 322-326.

Chrism Mass Homily of Pope Francis, March 28, 2013. http://www.vatican.va/holy_father/francesco/homilies/2013/documents/papa-francesco_20130328_messa-crismale_en.html (accessed March 29, 2013)

Ciancio, Antonella. "Pope Francis feted in Italian ancestral village." Reuters, March 15, 2013. (accessed March 23, 2013)

Collins, Roger. *Keepers of the Keys of Heaven: A History of the Papacy*. Basic Books, 2009.

Demacopoulos, George E. "The Extraordinary Historical Significance of His All-Holiness'
	Presence at Pope Francis' Installation as Bishop of Rome." Archon News. http://www.
	archons.org/news/detail.asp?id=619 (accessed March 28, 2013)

Dapelo, Santiago. "El éxtasis familiar por el 'loco de la guerra.'" www.lanacion.com,
	March 17, 2013. (accessed March 23, 2013)

De Vedia, Mariano. "Jorge Bergoglio, un sacerdote jesuita de Carrera." www.lanacion.com,
	March 13, 2013. (accessed March 23, 2013)

Donadio, Racherl. "Cardinals pick Bergoglio, who will be Pope Francis." *New York Times*,
	March 13, 2013.

Duffy, Eamon. *Saints & Sinners: A History of the Popes*. Yale University Press, 1997.

"El latín volvió a las misas." *Linea Capital*, September 17, 2007. http://www.lineacapital.
	com.ar/?noticia=31360 (accessed March 27, 2013)

Encarnacion, Omar. "The Catholic Crisis in Latin America." *Foreign Affairs*,
	March 19, 2013.

Fausset, Richard. "Pope Francis, the Buenos Aires pontiff." *Los Angeles Times*,
	March 16, 2013.

Frydlewski, Silvina and Anthony Faiola. "Beregoglio tested by Argentine leaders."
	Washington Post, March 14, 2013.

Ghosh, Palash R. "Pope Francis: A Friend to Muslims?" *International Business Times*,
	March 15, 2013.

Gray, Mark M. editor. "Catholicism in Spain." Center for Applied Research in the
	Apostolate (CARA). August 17, 2011.

Gray, Mark M., editor. "The Changing Jesuit Geography." Center for Applied Research
	in the Apostolate (CARA). February 1, 2011.

Gary, Mark M., editor. "Sunday Morning: Deconstructing Catholic Mass attendance in the
	1950s and now." Center for Applied Research in the Apostolate (CARA).
	August 17, 2011.

Glatz, Carol. "Pope washes young offenders' feet at Holy Thursday Mass." CatholicHerald.
	co.uk http://www.catholicherald.co.uk/news/2013/03/28/pope-washes-young-offend-
	ers-feet-at-holy-thursday-mass/ (accessed March 29, 2013)

Hebblethwaite, Margaret. "The Pope Francis I know." *Guardian*, March 14, 2013.

Hoffman, Matthew Cullinan. "Cardinal Archbishop of Buenos Aires rages against abortion "death sentence." LifeSitesNews.com, October 5, 2007. http://www.lifesitenews.com/news/archive//ldn/2007/oct/07100509 (accessed March 17, 2013)

The Holy See (www.vatican.va)

Hutchinson, John. "From fresh-faced schoolboy to leader of 1.2 billion Catholics: Charming images shed light on Pope Francis' early life growing up in Buenos Aires." The Mail Online, March 15, 2013. www.dailymail.co.uk (accessed March 23, 2013)

"Jorge Bergoglio y la sombra del gobierno military." Semana, March 14, 2013.

King, Ross. *Michelangelo & the Pope's Ceiling*. Walker & Company, 2003.

Mateucci, Piera. "Papa Francesco prega in Santa Maria Maggiore. Lombardi: 'Ha pagato il conto dell'albergo.' *La Repubblica*, March 14, 2013.

McGarry, Patsy. "'People's experience of church and the method of belonging' is set to change." IrishTimes.com, March 8, 2013.

Neuman, William. "'Dirty War' Victim Rejects Pope's Connection to Kidnapping." *New York Times*, March 21, 2013.

"New pope suffers for Argentine soccer club San Lorenzo." Reuters, March 13, 2013. http://sports.yahoo.com/news/pope-suffers-argentine-soccer-club-san-lorenzo-021844815--sow.html (accessed April 5, 2013).

Nossiter, Adam. "Church helps fill a void in Africa." New York Times, February 13, 2013.

O'Grady, Mary Anastasia. "Behind the Campaign to Smear the Pope." *Wall Street Journal*, March 17, 2013.

OSV Daily Take blog. www.osvdailytake.com

"Para Bergoglio, la ley matrimonio gay es 'una movida del Diablo.'" *Infobae*, July 8, 2010.

"Pope Francis 'a friend of the Islamic community.'" *Buenos Aires Herald*, March 14, 2013.

"Pope Francis backs Benedict's stand against relativism." CatholicCulture.org, March 22, 2013 http://www.catholicculture.org/news/headlines/index.cfm?storyid=17404 (accessed March 29, 2013)

"Pope Francis urges Catholics to 'search for the lost sheep' at first general audience." CatholicHerald.com.uk. March 27, 2013. http://www.catholicherald.co.uk/news/2013/03/27/pope-francis-urges-catholics-to-search-for-the-lost-sheep-at-first-general-audience/ (accessed March 29, 2013)

"Pope's Puppy Love Girlfriend Says he Always Wanted to be a Priest." Fox News Latino, March 15, 2013. http://latino.foxnews.com (accessed March 23, 2013)

Povoledo, Elisabetta. "Pope appeals for more interreligious dialogue." *New York Times*, March 22, 2013.

Reese, Thomas. "Francis, the Jesuits and the Dirty War." *National Catholic Reporter*, March 17, 2013.

Richards, Jeffrey. *The Popes and the Papacy in the Early Middle Ages 476–752*. Routledge & Kean, 1979.

Rubin, Sergio and Francesca Ambrogetti. *El Jesuita: Conversaciones con el cardenal Jorge Bergoglio, SJ*. Vergara, 2010.

Squires, Nick. "Pope Francis ditches red shoes." *Telegraph*, March 13, 2013.

Steffan, Melissa. Luis Palu: Why it matters that Pope Francis drinks mate with Evangelicals." *Christianity Today*, March 14, 2013.

Schwink, Taylor. "Kristallnacht remembered in Latin America." *Bnai Brith Magazine*, Spring 2013.

"Special Supplement: The Pope from the End of the World." *Clarin*, March 17, 2013. www.clarin.com.ar

US Conference of Catholic Bishops blog usccbmedia.blogspot.com

Weber, Jeremy. "Argentine Evangelicals say Bergoglio as Pope Francis is 'Answer to our prayers.'" *Christianity Today*, March 14, 2013.

Weigel, George. "Meeting Pope Francis." Institute on Religion and Democracy. http://juicyecumenism.com//?s=meeting+pope+francis&search=Go (accessed March 28, 2013)

White, Hilary. "Italy's Last Catholic Generation? Mass Attendance in "Collapse" among Under-30s." Lifesitesnews.com, August 9, 2010.

Weltin, E.G. *The Ancient Popes*. The Newman Press, 1964.

Whispers in the Loggia blog http://whispersintheloggia.blogspot.com

Wiker, Benjamin. "Benedict vs. the Dictatorship of Relativism." *National Catholic Register*, February 25, 2013. http://www.ncregister.com/blog/benjamin-wiker/benedict-vs.-the-dictatorship-of-relativism (accessed March 29, 2013)

Winfield, Nicole. "Pope reluctant to be pope: What does it mean?" Associated Press, March 27, 2013.

PICTURE CREDITS

ABOUT THE AUTHOR

Thomas J. Craughwell is author of more than forty books. Among them are, *Saints Behaving Badly* (Doubleday, 2006), *Popes Who Resigned* (TAN Books, 2013), and the forthcoming *St. Peter's Bones* (Image Books, 2014). Craughwell's book *Stealing Lincoln's Body* (Harvard University Press, 2007), has been adapted into a History Channel documentary.

Craughwell's articles have been printed in many journals and newspapers, including *The Wall Street Journal, The New York Times, Inside the Vatican*, and *Our Sunday Visitor*. A popular speaker, Craughwell is a Catholic Courses lecturer and has appeared on EWTN, CNN, and Ave Maria radio to discuss saints, the canonization process, and Catholic history. He writes out of his home in Bethel, Connecticut.